JUST FOR NEWLYWEDS

JUST FOR NEWLYWEDS

BRENT A. BARLOW

DESERET BOOK COMPANY
SALT LAKE CITY, UTAH

Library of Congress Cataloging-in-Publication Data

Barlow, Brent A., 1941–
    Just for newlyweds / Brent A. Barlow.
       p.   cm.
    Includes bibliographical references and index.
    ISBN 0-87579-623-0
    1. Marriage—Religious aspects—Christianity.   I. Title.
BV835.B343   1992
248.8′44—dc20
                  92-15334
                  CIP

Printed in the United States of America

10   9   8   7   6   5   4   3

To Susan,
with deep love and
appreciation

When a man hath taken a new wife, he shall not go out to war, neither shall he be charged with any business: but he shall be free at home one year, and shall cheer up his wife which he hath taken.

Deuteronomy 24:5

CONTENTS

ACKNOWLEDGMENTS

Many people contribute to publishing a book, and I wish to acknowledge and deeply thank those who have made this one a reality.

First, I would like to thank the numerous newlyweds at Brigham Young University who have been my students and shared with me their dreams and anxieties about marriage. These experiences stimulated my initial interest in writing *Just for Newlyweds*.

Second, my special thanks to Anne Pulley, Doug Moon, Tammi Hosman, and Cari Schreck, my teaching assistants at Brigham Young University during the past year, who have made insightful suggestions and assisted in proofreading the original manuscript. Thanks also to Chanalin Smith, receptionist in the Department of Family Sciences, for valuable suggestions. I also appreciate the support from Dr. Terrance Olson, Department Chairman, for his interest, encouragement, and friendship.

Third, I would like to thank the members of the BYU 33rd Ward, where I served as bishop during the writing and publication of this book. Most of them are newlyweds, and sharing with them their beginning years of marriage has been a wonderful experience. Ward members have made many valuable insights that have proven useful in my writing and teaching.

Fourth, special thanks to the staff at Deseret Book Company who have worked on this book. I appreciate very much the skills and talent of Richard

Tice, the editor for this book. Thanks also to Sheri Dew, Director of Publishing, and Ronald Millett, President of Deseret Book Company. I am indebted to the Deseret Book team who pitched in to produce *Just for Newlyweds:* Bronwyn Boyd, Richard Erickson, Craig Geertsen, Linda Nimori, Richard Peterson, Anne Sheffield, Patti Taylor, and Emily Watts.

Fifth, thanks to my children at home, who noticed and tolerated the fact that dad was somewhat detached while this book was being written.

And finally, to Susan, my wife, with whom I have awaited the sea gulls while fighting the crickets for twenty-seven years — to you I give special thanks and appreciation. Thank you for allowing me to write about a few of our experiences during our early years of marriage. Thank you for your patience while I worked on yet another book. If marriages are to succeed, indeed, "some must push, and some must pull." Thank you for doing both . . . and more than your share. May we continue to push and pull our load together for the remainder of the adventurous marital journey that lies ahead.

CHAPTER 1

INTRODUCTION

S uppose for a moment that you and your new husband or wife are planning to take a canoe trip. The trip will last several days, and you will cover about sixty miles. This canoe trip has been designed "just for newlyweds," and several hundred couples have signed up for the venture.

You meet in a large auditorium with the other couples to receive instructions on what to expect on your journey. You are excited. You hold hands as the guide begins his instructions.

The guide assures you that the journey is worthwhile. The canoes are sturdy. The currents in the river vary. The scenery will be beautiful in places and bland in others. Sometimes in the river you can just drift and still make progress. But there will also be rapids—white water—that can overturn your canoe. During these times you both must paddle with all your energy to keep your canoe from capsizing. More important during these turbulent times, both of you will have to learn to paddle together.

There is only one major problem with your canoe trip. The rapids and white water are very challenging during the first few miles, right after you have begun. As inexperienced river runners, you will immediately experience difficult times. In fact, your guide states that he wants to give you the success and failure rates of those who have begun the trip before.

* More than half who have recently begun the sixty-mile journey together did not finish. With the new spring run-off that has added to the rapids, as many as two-thirds may not finish on this particular expedition.

* Of those who do not finish, 54 percent will quit during the first five miles when they are least experienced and the rapids are very swift.

The guide stops and reiterates the challenges and difficulties that await you at the beginning of the journey. (Surely, you think, these trends and statistics apply to everyone else. But not to you. The two of you will be among those who make it. You give your partner's hand a gentle squeeze.) Your guide reassures you that the trip is worthwhile, but he wants you to know what to expect. He asks you to go home and discuss what he has told you. What equipment are you going to take? Do you both know how to paddle a canoe? What skills do each of you have in managing a canoe in rapids? Will you be able to row together when necessary during difficult times? Or, will each of you be paddling in different directions? And now that you both know something of the danger right at the beginning, what will you do differently from what you had planned? What new plans will you make? What precautions will you take before you begin? And if you do tip over, will you give up? Or will you get back in your canoe and continue the journey?

Marriage and canoe trips — is there an analogy? Could we compare sixty years of marriage to a sixty-mile canoe trip?

LAUNCHING OURSELVES INTO SPACE

Let's make one other comparison. Almost all of us have watched at some time the astronauts circling the earth in their spacecraft. Through television and video cameras within the spacecraft, we have been able to watch them work and play in space. We have watched in awe at the seemingly effortless ease with which they walked in space and, years ago, even landed and walked on the moon.

Few of us are aware, however, of the long hours of preparation that astronauts make for their space flights. Furthermore, many of us do not often think of or realize the eminent danger that faces the astronauts as they are launched from earth. Truly, the most dangerous part of the space mission is during the first few minutes when astronauts are strapped into their seats, gases are ignited, lift-off begins, and the craft is thrust into space. The immediate danger of such missions was vividly demonstrated on January 26, 1986, when the spacecraft *Challenger* blasted off from Cape Kennedy in Florida. With the whole world watching by television, we joyfully applauded as the spacecraft left the earth. But, in just a few minutes when it was barely into orbit, the spacecraft exploded, and the entire crew was consumed in a giant fireball.

A wedding ceremony and reception are also joyful occasions. Family, neighbors, friends, and photographers gather to witness the launching and celebrate the wedding of the couple. There are even photographs in the newspaper. But what begins as a joyful and happy occasion can end up as a disaster. There is especially great danger during the first few years of marriage, right at the beginning, during lift-off.

Young couples need to prepare better and need more help during the initial phase of their marriage. With this in mind, I have written *Just for Newlyweds*. Perhaps this book can serve as a travel guide for those who have recently married or who are about to do so. Let me be your guide and point out both the beautiful scenery and the rapids that lie ahead. I will share with you some of the experiences Susan and I had during our early years of marriage as we learned (and are still learning!) to paddle our canoe. We too hit the rapids and white water fairly early in our marital journey.

I hope young couples who read this book will commit or recommit to the journey, make the necessary preparations, strap on their life jackets, and

3

enjoy the scenery along the way. Even though the initial rapids are dangerous, they can also be exhilarating and exciting. Modern revelation declares, "If ye are prepared ye shall not fear." (D&C 38:30.) So, prepare . . . and enjoy the journey. You can learn to paddle together in the rapids and white water of marriage . . . no matter how many miles you have traveled.

In Deuteronomy 24:5 we read: "When a man hath taken a new wife, he shall not go out to war, neither shall he be charged with any business: but he shall be free at home one year, and shall cheer up his wife which he hath taken." Why was a young husband in ancient Israel not required to perform military duty during the first year of his marriage? Why was he cautioned not to become excessively involved with business or other pursuits during that important first year? Why was he admonished to stay home and be with his new wife during that time? What did the ancients know about the early years of marriage that we may not have yet learned, or perhaps failed to recognize? And finally, is the wisdom of the ancients still relevant today?

MARRIAGE TRENDS FOR THE 1990S

Few things are more exciting or uplifting than a wedding ceremony and reception for a young couple. For many, the wedding is a time of reunion as family members and friends gather together to wish the newlyweds well. Tears frequently flow as the bride and groom exchange wedding vows of commitment and loyalty. At the reception later that afternoon or evening, the new bride and groom are warmly embraced as those attending offer congratulations. The proud parents, the bridesmaids, and the groom's attendants all stand in the reception line to greet the guests. Many give gifts to help the newly married couple become established in life. After the guests are received, there is usually the traditional "getaway" as the bride and groom leave the assembled crowd to commence their life together. This wedding-day scenario, or something very similar, is repeated more than two million times each year in the United States. (In 1988, there were 2,400,000 marriages in the U.S. In Utah, there were 16,759 marriages in 1987, the last year for which statistics are available.) But what happens to these couples as they embark on their precarious journeys in life? What do many of these young men and women experience shortly after they have made serious vows and commitments to be and stay together?

Early in 1990, I was asked to address the Association of Mormon Counselors and Psychotherapists (AMCAP) at their spring convention in Salt Lake City. The title of my speech was "Strengthening Marriage: Current Status and Expectations for the Decade of the 1990s." In preparing for my talk, I reviewed some of the some current trends that likely will continue into the future.

Regarding marriage, it appears that over 93 percent of the population in the United States will marry. The median age for first marriages is about 23.6 for women and 26.7 for men. Marriage continues to be one of the most popular voluntary endeavors in the United States today. No one has to marry, but just about everyone does. Getting married and having children tend to be dominant life goals in the U.S. regardless of race, religion, or ethnic identity. Even among those who divorce, 67 percent of the women and 75 percent of the men eventually remarry. In the LDS Church, marriage is understandably even more popular. Approximately 97 percent of Latter-day Saints eventually marry.

At the AMCAP meeting, I also talked about some divorce trends in the United States. Among those couples who married in the 1940s, about 24 percent are expected to divorce. Men and women marrying in the 1950s and 60s can expect a divorce rate of about 36 percent. But a pronounced shift in divorce occurred among those who have married since 1970. The majority, 53–56 percent of these couples, are now expected to legally terminate their marriage, making separation the rule rather than the exception. (See Arthur J. Norton and Jeanne E. Moorman, "Current Trends in Marriage and Divorce among American Women," *Journal of Marriage and the Family* 49 [February 1987]: 3–14.)

Dr. Tim Heaton, sociologist at Brigham Young University, has noted:

> *What the latest statistics do show is that two-thirds of the couples who married in the United States for the first time in the 1980s can expect to divorce.* For many, this seems unbelievably high. What this figure takes into account is the divorce statistics for the 1980s. The figure currently tossed around is a 50 percent chance of divorce—much lower than the two-thirds rate. But what people don't know is that the statistic is based on data compiled up to 1979. It does not take the '80s into account. . . .
>
> For LDS couples the total rate of divorce is approximately 20 percent below the national average. In the mid 1980s, when the last survey was taken, it was estimated that 35 percent of all LDS marriages would end in divorce. [The BYU demographer suspects this has risen and probably now lies somewhere between 40 to 50 percent for the LDS Church as a whole.] LDS Temple marriages are one-fifth as likely to end in divorce as nontemple marriages, although this too has probably risen since the last survey was completed in 1981. (In Carri P. Jenkins, "The Changing Family," *BYU Today,* March 1990, pp. 26–31; italics added. For additional information on LDS divorce trends prior to 1981, see Tim B. Heaton and Kristen L. Goodman, "LDS Church Members in the U.S. and Canada: A Demographic Profile," *AMCAP Journal* 12, no. 1 [1986]: 88–107; and *Church News,* Nov. 6, 1983.)

Remember, divorces rates of 50–67 percent for some age groups during the decade ahead are just projections and estimates. But what if they turn out to be accurate? As I suggested at the AMCAP convention, forget the exact figures. Simply stated, a large number of married couples in the United States today, perhaps the majority, will become divorced.

I also reviewed some of the trends of divorce in Utah. In 1990, there were 8,950 divorces, up from 8,110 in 1989. Apparently many divorces occur in the early years of marriage. A careful examination of divorces in Utah by duration of marriage during the years 1980-87 reveals some alarming trends:

DURATION OF MARRIAGE	% OF DIVORCES*	CUMULATIVE %
Less than 1 year	7.3	7.3
1st year	11.0	18.3
2nd year	11.0	29.3
3rd year	9.2	38.5
4th year	8.0	46.5
5th year	7.0	53.5
6th–10th years	20.5	74.0
11th–15th years	10.5	84.5
16th–19th years	4.8	89.3
20th–24th years	3.9	93.2
25th–29th years	2.0	95.2
30th–34th years	1.1	96.3
35th–39th years	1.0	97.3
40 years plus	.4	97.7
Not stated	2.3	100.0

*Includes annulments

(*Utah's Vital Statistics*, Technical Report No. 146, February 1992, and 1988 Annual Report, Bureau of Vital Records and Health Statistics, Utah Department of Health, Salt Lake City, Utah.)

From these statistics the following five points are worth noting:

1. Approximately 7 percent of divorces in Utah occur before one year of marriage.

2. The highest divorce rates in Utah are in the first and second year, when eleven percent of the divorces occur each year.

3. Thirty-eight percent of Utah's divorces are granted to couples married three years or less. This follows a trend in the United States for the divorce rate to peak after three years of marriage. (See Frank D. Cox, "The Dissolution of Marriage," in *Human Intimacy: Marriage, the Family and Its Meaning,* 5th ed. [New York City: West Publishing, 1990], p. 553.)

4. Over half (nearly 54 percent) of Utah's divorces occur within the first five years of marriage.

5. There are relatively few divorces after ten years of marriage in Utah. Seventy-four percent of the divorces have occurred by the tenth year; 84 percent by the fifteenth year; and approximately 90 percent by the twentieth year. Only ten percent of the divorces in Utah occur after twenty years of marriage.

One other interesting trend is evident from the statistical reports. People in the western and southern areas of the United States appear to divorce earlier than in other areas. Couples in the U.S. divorce at a *median* of about seven years of marriage. But the statistics vary according to geographical areas, with residents of some states divorcing earlier.

Couples in the eastern part of the United States (Massachusetts, Pennsylvania, Rhode Island, Connecticut, and Vermont) apparently wait longer, a seven to eight year *median,* to divorce. Other states, however (Alaska, Alabama, Wyoming, Kansas, Utah, Georgia, Idaho, Kentucky, Tennessee, and Montana), have a *median* of five to six years to divorce. In 1979, Utah and Wyoming led the nation in the shortest duration of marriage until divorce, each with a median of 4.8 years!

I wonder why couples in the Intermountain West opt for divorces some two years earlier than those living in the eastern part of the United States. Are they less patient? Less committed? Do they give up too early, comparatively speaking, when trying to make their marriages work?

At the conclusion of my talk at the AMCAP Convention, I suggested that during the decade of the 90s in the United States, we would likely continue to see (1) the vast majority of people getting married, (2) over half getting divorced, and (3) most of the divorces occurring within the first few years of married life. What impact these current trends will have on LDS marriages, both temple and nontemple, remains to be seen.

One of the proposals I made was that we needed to give greater aid and support to newlyweds and couples in the early years of marriage. We can help stabilize these marriages, which in the beginning stages are apparently so vulnerable to disruption. By so doing, we might also reverse some of the monumental divorce trends projected for the next decade. This book, *Just for Newlyweds,* is a contribution to my own proposal.

CHAPTER 2

THE TRANSITION TO MARRIAGE

Making the transition from "I" to "we" can be a rewarding and yet somewhat frustrating experience. During our single years, we become accustomed to doing things in our own way, in our own time, and at our own unique pace. But after we marry, we are expected to suddenly merge into a "oneness," a union, a couple identity to which we are not accustomed. And this transition is often expected to be done quickly, even immediately, right after the wedding. Seldom does it occur like that. Following are a few thoughts that may aid newlyweds to make that all important transition in life, from being single . . . to being married.

A STRANGE AND WONDERFUL RELATIONSHIP

I was talking to a young husband not long ago who had been married less than a year. In half-jest he said, "My wife and I have a strange and wonderful relationship. She's strange and I'm wonderful!"

What the young man said somewhat jokingly is true of almost all marital relationships. We go through an early stage in which we don't understand some of the things he or she does. "If only my sweetheart would do this" or "If only my sweetheart could be like me" we sometimes wonder silently or even out loud.

Some research indicates that a major transition occurs in the last half of the first year, when couples begin to reassess their marital relationships. During dating, engagement, and the first six months of marriage, the couple experience an extended honeymoon of sorts. It is a highly romantic period, with emphasis on the ideal. Spouses overlook each other's shortcomings or do not even notice them because of the emotional ecstasy they are experiencing. That's partly because people tend to marry what they wish the other person to be. That is, people marry the fantasy they have of each other. But that ideal image lasts only for a short period of time.

During the years I have been at Brigham Young University, I have taught a marriage enhancement class for engaged or married couples. Observing the couples who enroll in the course is quite interesting. Fiancés and newly married couples don't think that any of the things we discuss pertain to them. The couples married nearly a year or more, however, are quite different. Reality has set in for them, and they are aware of both their own and their spouses' imperfections.

This is the period when many couples try to change each other. They will often use the three Ds of change: the demand ("If you don't _____, I will _____), the demonstration ("If you loved me, you would _____), or the deal ("I will do _____, if you will do _____.") Such couples are what I refer to as the Gruesome Twosomes. Probably nothing is more frustrating than two married people trying to change each other to meet their own idiosyncratic wants.

About this time, couples will come across something like "The Rules of Marriage." Someone sent them to me not long ago, and I don't know who the author is. Susan likes them and thinks we should adopt them. I think we already have.

Rule #1: The wife always makes the rules.

Rule #2: The rules are subject to change at any time without prior notification.

Rule #3: No husband can possibly know all the rules.

Rule #4: If the wife suspects that the husband knows all the rules, she must immediately change some of them.

Rule #5: The wife is never wrong.

Rule #6: If the wife is wrong, it is because of a flagrant misunderstanding that resulted directly from something the husband did or said.

Rule #7: If Rule #6 applies, the husband must apologize immediately for causing the misunderstanding.

Rule #8: The wife can change her mind at any given time.

Rule #9: The husband must never change his mind without express written consent from the wife.

Rule #10: The wife has every right to be angry or upset at any time.

Rule #11: The husband must remain calm at all times, unless the wife wants him to be angry or upset.

Rule #12: The wife must under no circumstances let the husband know whether or not she wants him to be angry or upset.

THE PYGMALION SYNDROME

I remember a conversation I had with a young man some time ago who was not getting along with his wife. He said she was not willing to follow his advice. I asked why.

"I give her advice on how she can improve on what she is doing," he reported. "I tell her how she can be a better woman and spouse." Then he casually mentioned, "I believe it is the husband's responsibility to train and educate his wife."

"You mean a husband and wife should be willing to learn from one another," I suggested.

"No, not learn from each other. The man is supposed to educate his wife."

I thought for a moment and then asked, somewhat humorously, "When was the last time you saw *My Fair Lady?*"

The movie, released in 1956, was based on the play *Pygmalion*, written by George Bernard Shaw in 1912. The theme of the play and movie was "Women are the creations of men." The play itself was based on the Greek legend of Pygmalion, king of Cyprus, who became disgusted with the women of his day and carved an ivory statue of a beautiful woman. Then he fell in love with his creation—the statue. In answer to his prayer, the goddess Aphrodite made the statue into a living woman named Galatea, whom Pygmalion later married.

The suggestion that men create women brought back vivid memories of *My Fair Lady*. In the movie, Henry Higgins struggled with Eliza Doolittle, trying to "help" her overcome her cockney accent and elevate her to an unfamiliar standard of living. To express his frustrations, Dr. Higgins sang, "Why Can't a Woman Be More Like a Man?" His triumphant delight was the moment at a gala ball when Eliza descended the staircase in her elegant gown.

The young husband thought for a moment and then suggested that the Greek legend reflected an accurate principle: Women become what they are through the efforts of men. I asked, however, if the opposite was also true. Men are what their wives help them become. I reminded him of the old adage that every woman has two husbands: the one she is given, and the one she creates. He disagreed and suggested that it was improper for a woman to "train and educate her husband in anything."

The struggling husband held a common but outdated and misleading belief: that men are, by nature, superior to women. If he did believe that men

13

know more and have superior intellect, logic, and judgment, I better understood why he was struggling, and I also better understood his wife's frustration.

For years, the "male superior" concept has been a major cause of marital disruption and dissatisfaction in America. Of course, some men are more capable than some women in some things. But the opposite is also true. Some women are more capable than some men in some things. Marriage is not a battle of the sexes. Every individual has some skills and attributes that others do not possess, and every spouse is skilled in areas that the other is not, regardless of being male or female.

The rigid male-centered marriage of the past few hundred years will not survive during the next decade or into the twenty-first century. Newlyweds, particularly the young husbands, should not become preoccupied with who has the right to do what to whom—and when. A marital relationship, to survive in the future, must be built, not on superiority, but on equality, mutual responsibility, security, and dignity.

HAPPINESS RESULTS FROM MAKING CHOICES

According to a recent Gallup Poll, 65 percent of college coeds interviewed wanted to marry, be mothers, and have full-time employment. In a way, this is understandable. After all, a young man can marry, be a father, and have full-time employment. Does it follow, though, that a young wife can both be a mother and be employed full-time, and still maintain her sanity? And will all this make her happy?

During the past several years, I have been able to talk to hundreds of people about their concerns in life. Many of the women were very talented and genuinely cared about their husbands and children. But some of them were not happy with either their marriages or life in general. Some desired

14

experiences in other realms of life that often included employment. Others wanted to be wives and mothers at home but secretly envied employed women.

For some time I thought that the answer to these marital concerns was for husbands to help wives explore a few mountain peaks beyond the home. For many couples, it meant full- or part-time employment for the wife.

But I soon realized that such an answer addressed only part of the problem. Many wives and mothers who were already employed outside the home, either full- or part-time, were equally unhappy with life. And their marriages were suffering. Many of these women silently resented the fact that they were at work. Some, I might add, suffered a great deal of stress and fatigue by having to work yet still having to perform many of the household tasks with little or no help from husbands or children. Many of these women expressed a need to have more help at home. Some wanted to quit work and be home with their children. Others wanted a periodic break from the hectic pace of being mothers, wives, and employees — they simply needed a rest.

This disparity continued to puzzle me for some time. Many wives were not happy being solely at home, yet other women were not content with outside employment. This situation is a concern because more than 90 percent of married women are expected to be employed at some time during their married life.

Finally, I realized that the issue was not so much whether wives were employed or stayed at home. The women I have found to be most content with life are those who have been able to make choices as to where they want to be and what they want to do. Women who choose to stay at home seem to be the most happy, as are those women who choose to be employed. The real discontentment and dissatisfaction with life seem to come for women who are forced, by one means or another, to do either one.

Not long ago in a church meeting, the congregation sang the hymn "Know This, That Every Soul Is Free." (*Hymns*, 1985, no. 240.) During the service I read it several times. Then, in my mind I changed several words so that the first three verses read as follows:

Know this, that ev'ry woman should be free,
To choose her life and what she'll be;
For this eternal truth is giv'n:
That God will force no woman to heav'n.

He'll call, persuade, direct aright,
And bless with wisdom, love, and light,
In nameless ways be good and kind,
But never force the human mind.

Freedom and reason make us women;
Take these away, what are we then?
Mere animals, and just as well
The beasts may think of heav'n or hell.

In order for anyone to be happy, they must have the freedom to make choices in life. This is particularly true for newlyweds as they begin their married life together. As singles, they made most or all of their own choices. Now, as couples, they must be able to continue using their reasoning capabilities to choose from many alternatives.

MARRIAGE REQUIRES BOTH COURAGE AND FEAR

Recently in my classes at BYU, I reviewed all the dismal statistics about what is happening to many marriages in the United States. But my students seemed undaunted. They cautiously but eagerly awaited marriage.

Marrying at the present time takes a great deal of courage. Some students come from homes where their parents' marriages were not the best. In addition,

16

many have what I call "guarded skepticism" about getting married. They are acutely aware of the jungle-like atmosphere in which many marriages are struggling. BYU students today do not naïvely sing and dance down the proverbial yellow brick road on the way to the emerald city of matrimony. Most are wise in regards to current marriage trends and values. Yet still, they all look forward to marriage.

Some admit that they feel strong social pressure from a variety of sources to marry. Even though they individually make the final decision when, where, and whom to marry, they feel pressure to take the plunge. And once they do, I'm amazed at how many of them do succeed at marriage when there are so many opportunities, if you will, to fail.

I am not certain, however, whether young people today are motivated in marriage by (1) courage to succeed or (2) the fear of failure. Perhaps both. There is a difference between the two, though a popular joke about courage and fear illustrates that the result can be the same:

A wealthy man invited some of his associates to see his new ranch in Arizona. After touring the mountains, rivers, and grasslands, he took everyone back to the house, which was just as spectacular. Behind the exquisite home was the largest swimming pool in all of Arizona. There was another thing about it, however, that was even more unusual. The pool was filled with alligators.

The rich owner explained that he valued courage more than any other character trait. Courage, he claimed, was what had made him a billionaire. "In fact, I value courage so much that if anyone is courageous enough to jump in that pool, swim through those alligators, and make it to the other side, I'll give them anything they want—my house, my land, my money."

Of course, everyone laughed at the absurd challenge. Suddenly they heard a splash. Turning around, they saw a young man swimming for his life across the pool as the alligators swarmed after him.

17

After several death-defying seconds, the young man made it unharmed to the other side. The host and his guests applauded his efforts, and the billionaire said to him, "You are indeed a man of courage, and I will stick to my word. You can have anything—my house, my land, my money. Just tell me what you want."

The young swimmer breathed heavily for a few moments, then said, "I want to know just one thing. Who pushed me into that pool?"

To young couples recently married, I applaud your courage and understand your fear now that you have jumped—or been nudged—into matrimony. My only advice is this: Now that you are in, commit to exerting all efforts and proceed with haste to get past the dangers safely.

President Spencer W. Kimball wrote this about commitment:

> While one is young and well and strong and beautiful or handsome and attractive, he or she can (for the moment) almost name the price and write the ticket; but the time comes when these temporary things have had their day; when wrinkles come and aching joints; when hair is thin and bodies bulge; when nerves are frayed and tempers are taut; when wealth is dissipated. . . .
>
> There comes a time when those who flattered us and those whose wit and charm deceived us may leave us to our fate. Those are times when we want friends, good friends, common friends, loved ones, tied with immortal bonds—people who will nurse our illnesses, tolerate our eccentricities, and love us with pure, undefiled affection. Then we need an unspoiled companion who will not count our wrinkles, remember our stupidities nor remember our weaknesses; then is when we need a loving companion with whom we have suffered and wept and prayed and worshipped; one with whom we have suffered sorrow and disappointments, one who loves us for what we are or intend to be rather than what we

18

appear to be in our gilded shell. (Edward L. Kimball, ed., *The Teachings of Spencer W. Kimball* [Salt Lake City: Bookcraft, 1982], p. 310.)

RECOMMITMENT SOMETIMES NECESSARY

Is it appropriate for husbands and wives to recommit to each other on occasion? Some say not, that when you marry, you make your vows and commitments at that time, and thus making them again is unnecessary. Others, however, feel that husbands and wives should let each other know that they still hold to their original wedding vows.

In my marriage enhancement classes, I encourage young couples to periodically recommit to each other. I think it is particularly significant during the early years of marriage because a high number of divorces occur during the first three or four years. I tell my students that on our wedding anniversary on June 5, Susan and I like to go out to celebrate one more year together and to recommit for the next.

Apparently a few of the students were listening. Not long ago I received the following letter:

Dear Dr. Barlow:

My husband and I will have been married four years in December. The first semester we were married, we took your class on marriage enrichment at BYU. We enjoyed it very much. One thing we remember and still use from your class is the phrase "I recommit." We say this to one another frequently. We felt at the time that we had an unusually strong and committed union. This has proven to be more than true. During the ups and downs and some very stressful times during our four years, we have remained very much in love and very committed to one another.

My husband is the kind who would sit up all night with me if I were sick, and more. He gets up with the baby at all hours, plus every morning so I can sleep in. He washes all the dishes because he knows I hate that particular chore. He tells me he loves me at least five times a day. He cleans the house and bakes better than I do. He is sensitive and tender and always concerned with making me happy. I really can't say enough about how wonderful he is! I can't imagine what I ever did to deserve him, but I thank Heavenly Father every day for a husband like him.

Of course our marriage isn't perfect. But these are some things we do to strengthen our commitment: Every anniversary we write letters to each other of love, gratitude, etc., and seal them up. We open them the next year, and write new ones. We touch each other often in nondemanding ways. It is hard to not be emotionally close to someone when you are touching. We talk a lot. And not just about the weather. We try and get at a feeling level every day, even if briefly. This again helps keep that emotional closeness that I feel is vital for true commitment. We spend a lot of time together. We go to bed together. We pray together.

Commitment in marriage isn't one big thing—it is many little things. And for me, it is that amazing feeling of being able to completely trust myself to another person in every way, without fear of being let down or deceived. Thank you for letting me share these thoughts with you.

I, in turn, thank a former student for writing. As most teachers are aware, knowing that something you have taught may have made a difference in a person's life is a wonderful reward. As the letter illustrates, husband and wives, both young and old, should periodically recommit to travel life's journey together. Old promises can be made new, and stale relationships can be made fresh. Such is commitment in contemporary married life.

. . . .

CHAPTER 3

SING AND DANCE TOGETHER

A s noted in the introduction, ancient wisdom encouraged newlyweds not to get involved in so many day-to-day affairs that their married life was disrupted. (See Deut. 24:5.) The insight is also good for those married a few years as well.

OVERLOADING YOUR MARRIAGE

In his book *Love for a Lifetime: Building a Marriage That Will Go the Distance,* Dr. James C. Dobson, a Christian psychologist, responded to the question, What are the major "marriage killers" in contemporary marriage? His answer should be of particular interest to those recently married. He wrote:

> *Overcommitment and physical exhaustion.* Beware of this danger. It is especially insidious for young couples who are trying to get started in a profession or in school. Do *not* try to go to college, work full-time, have a baby, manage a toddler, fix up a house and start a business at the same time. It sounds ridiculous, but many young couples do just that and are then surprised when their marriage falls apart. Why wouldn't it? The only time they see each other is when they are worn out! It is especially dangerous to have the husband vastly overcommitted and the wife staying home with a preschooler. Her profound loneliness builds discontent and depression, and we all know where that leads. You must reserve time for one another

21

if you want to keep your love alive. (Portland, Oregon: Multnomah Press, 1987, p. 107.)

What are some of the stresses and strains taking heavy tolls on contemporary society? A few years ago, writer and researcher Delores Curran surveyed over six hundred people to find out. In her book *Stress and the Healthy Family* (Minneapolis: Winston Press, Inc., 1985), she reported that married women indicated the following ten items as top stresses, in order of priority:

1. Economics/finances/budgeting
2. Lack of shared responsibility in the family
3. Insufficient couple time
4. Children's behavior/discipline/sibling fighting
5. Housekeeping standards
6. Insufficient "me" time
7. Guilt for not accomplishing more
8. Insufficient family playtime
9. Spousal relationship (communication, friendship, sex)
10. Self-image/self-esteem/feelings of unattractiveness

Likewise, what were the top ten stresses, again in order of priority, for husbands?

1. Economics/finances/budgeting
2. Insufficient couple time
3. Communicating with children
4. Children's behavior/discipline/sibling fighting
5. Spousal relationship (communication, friendship, sex)
6. Overscheduled family calendar
7. Insufficient "me" time
8. Unhappiness with work situation
9. Insufficient family playtime

10. Television (Pp. 20–21.)

Dr. Dobson's observation of the #1 marriage killer and Delores Curran's research findings strongly suggest that being involved in too many things or projects, with the fatigue and exhaustion that follow, is a major factor in marital disruption today.

Note also that in the two lists above, the stresses for wives are not always the same as the stresses for husbands. A husband and wife may share the same house, the same children, and the same daily routines yet experience all of them quite differently. Because of these differences, husbands and wives should become aware of each other's concerns and problems. Couples can then more fully accomplish their responsibility to "bear one another's burdens" and "comfort those that stand in need of comfort." (Mosiah 18:8–9.)

RELIEVING THE OVERLOAD

Married couples who bear burdens and stresses well, according to Dolores Curran, do the following:

1. The healthy couple views stress as a normal part of family life.
2. The healthy couple shares feelings as well as words.
3. The healthy couple develops conflict-resolution skills and creative coping skills.
4. The healthy couple makes use of support people and systems.
5. The healthy couple is adaptable. (See pp. 28–50 for an extensive report of these findings.)

As newlyweds, what will you do when the stress and strains of life come? What will you do when your canoe hits the white water in the rapids? Almost all married couples have experiences that, in one form or another, test their marriages. What will you do when they occur for you?

A key to success is to learn not to "run faster or labor more than you have strength and means." (D&C 10:4.) How are you going to learn to conserve your strength and energy? How are you going to judge what you can and cannot handle in life?

What people do to relax and enjoy life varies from person to person and from time to time. Some like to participate in various sports. Others enjoy theater, concerts, or plays. Crafts and hobbies, reading, deep-breathing exercises, working in the yard or garden—these have all helped some people unwind. Some like writing letters or writing in journals and diaries. Hot tubs, saunas, or Jacuzzi help others relax, while walks in the park or scenic trips to the woods, mountains, or desert help others. Some like to play musical instruments, while others enjoy naps or sunbathing at the beach. Prayer, scripture reading, or meditation help some re-create, while movies or quiet music are helpful to others. Some like to play with young children. Others enjoy the company of animals. And yes, others like to sing and dance.

An insight on this is found in the Doctrine and Covenants. On January 14, 1847, the Lord gave his word and will through President Brigham Young for the massive movement of the Saints westward. This revelation was recorded as section 136. The journey appeared to be a difficult one. They were to organize into companies numbering ten, fifty, and one hundred, with a captain of each. (See v. 3.) They were all to share equally in assisting the widows and the fatherless. (See v. 8.) They were to keep their pledges with each other and not covet what they did not have. (See v. 20.) They were commanded to not contend with one another or speak evil of each other, to cease drunkenness, to return what they had borrowed, and to search diligently for what might be lost. (See vv. 23–26.)

Finally, in verse twenty-eight, they were commanded to praise the Lord with singing and dancing on the journey. Now the key question: Why did the Lord command the early Saints to sing and dance during the arduous journey westward?

Put yourself in their place. You have been driving a team of oxen or mules all day in the hot weather. Or perhaps you have been riding in the back of a jostling, stuffy wagon, tending little children for ten or twelve hours. Perhaps either you or your spouse has walked much of the distance that day, maybe twenty miles or more. It is now nighttime. All in the family are tired and hungry. After the evening meal—which is almost the same as all the meals you've had for several weeks—you are ready for bed. While you are thinking of the much-needed rest that awaits you, you hear someone tuning up a fiddle near the central campfire. "Oh, no," you think to yourself. "Not that again." Yes, it is that time. The evening dance is about to begin!

I have often wondered why the Lord commanded the Saints to sing and dance while they were crossing the plains. One would imagine that he would say, "Conserve your strength," or "Get as much rest as you can." But no, come evening or when any other opportunity arose, they were to sing and dance. Why?

Maybe this tells us something about the importance of balance in life. Maybe it has to do with the fact that recreation is often a form of re-creation. In his discourse at the temple, King Benjamin noted that "it is not requisite that a man should run faster than he has strength." (Mosiah 4:27.) In the latter days, the Prophet Joseph Smith had a great work to perform that required great physical and emotional strength. The Lord gave Joseph the same counsel that Benjamin gave his people. (See D&C 10:4.) Apparently Joseph learned how to relax and unwind as the need arose. One associate noted:

> At that time Joseph was studying Greek and Latin, and when he got tired studying he would go and play with the children in their games about

25

the house, to give himself exercise. Then he would go back to his studies as before.

He was preaching once, and he said it tried some of the pious folks to see him play ball with the boys. He then related a story of a certain prophet who was sitting under the shade of a tree amusing himself in some way, when a hunter came along with his bow and arrow, and reproved him. The prophet asked him if he kept his bow strung up all the time. The hunter answered that he did not. The prophet asked why, and he said it would lose its elasticity if he did. The prophet said it was just so with his mind, he did not want it strung up all the time. ("Recollections of the Prophet Joseph Smith," *Juvenile Instructor* 27 (1892): 302, 472.)

Note also that in June 1850, just three years after the pioneers arrived in Utah, the first theatrical play was performed in the Bowery on Temple Square. Why do you think President Brigham Young placed such emphasis on drama, literature, and the arts and, yes, continued to emphasize singing and dancing during those early and often difficult years of conquering the Western deserts? Two of his daughters later quoted their father as saying:

Life is best enjoyed when time periods are evenly divided between labour, sleep and recreation. All men, women and children should labour; all must sleep; and if mental and physical balance is to be maintained, all people should spend one-third of their time in recreation, which is re-building, voluntary activity — never idleness. 'Eight hours work, eight hours sleep, and eight hours recreation' was Brigham Young's motto. *Re-creation* is indeed the meaning of recreation. (Susa Young Gates and Leah D. Widtsoe, *The Life Story of Brigham Young* [New York: The Macmillan Company, 1931], p. 251.)

The author Robert Fulghum gives this observation a contemporary setting. He claims dancing is essential to a well-rounded life:

When I get down and my life is logjammed and I need some affirmative action, I go where people dance. I don't mean joints where people go to get crocked and then wobble around on the floor to music. I mean places where people who really like to dance go to do that. I like dancers. Never met a serious dancer who wasn't a pretty fine human being. And I enjoy the never-ending pleasure of being surprised by just who dancers are. . . . All this reminds me of something I heard about the Hopi Indians. They don't think there is much difference between praying and dancing—that both are necessary for a long life. . . . They say that to be a useful Hopi is to be one who has a quiet heart and takes part in all the dances. (*It Was on Fire When I Lay Down on It* [New York: Villard Books, 1990], pp. 46, 49.)

As newlyweds, it really does not matter if you don't like to sing and dance. What is important is that you find some ways to relax, to re-create in your own unique ways, both as a young couple and as individuals. Hopefully, you will learn early in your marriage not to overcommit to too many activities. Hugh Nibley has noted that "the challenge of Latter-day Saints is not only to choose between good and evil; we also have to learn to choose between good and good." There are just too many good causes to champion in life. We can burn up all our strength and energy with too many good ones as well as a few bad ones. The goal is not to become so committed to so many things in life that we don't have the time or energy for loving, caring relationships.

Newlyweds would do well to follow the admonitions of an anonymous Irish poet who wrote

Take time for work.	It is the price of success.
Take time to think.	It is the source of power.
Take time to play.	It is the secret of youth.
Take time to read.	It is the foundation of wisdom.

Take time to be friendly.	It is the road to happiness.
Take time to dream.	It is hitching your wagon to a star.
Take time to love.	It is the highest joy in life.
Take time to laugh.	It is the music of the soul.

And I would add:

| Take time to pray. | It is the pathway to eternity. |

There should be balance in our lives: "To every thing there is a season, and a time to every purpose under the heaven: . . . a time to laugh . . . and a time to dance." (Eccl. 3:1, 3.)

CHAPTER 4

MARRIAGE MYTHS

I n one class I taught on the early years of marriage, a young coed observed in her term paper, "Everyone looks for the perfect marriage partner, and while looking, they get married." It is true that everyone would like to have a perfect marriage. And that would necessitate having a perfect marriage partner and being perfect ourselves. While many of us believe ourselves to be the personification of perfection itself during our dating years, romantic love, especially when fueled by sexual passion, tricks us into thinking that the perfect marriage is in the making. After marriage we find that this is not so, that both partners are mere mortals. Not long ago another student had this insight: "We need idealism tempered with realism in marriage."

Susan and I like to go to movies. For us, it is an escape from the hectic pressures of home and life. I've noted an interesting phenomenon with respect to movie-going. A new movie is released with the usual hype and advertising. We believe the hoopla and go. But often after we see the movie, I feel somewhat let down. The movie is usually entertaining, but sometimes the expectation is so great that there is a let-down after viewing the film.

There is a word for this phenomenon. It is called cognitive dissonance. It is simply the difference between what we expect and what we experience. Sometimes if the expectations are excessively high, there is great dissonance, or disappointment, no matter how high the level of experience or performance.

MYTHS ABOUT MARRIAGE

Most marriage and family counselors and educators believe that there are many myths about marriage. In other words, society harbors many excessive or unrealistic expectations about marriage. This is particularly significant since people usually act on what they believe to be true. More than thirty marriage myths have been identified by various researchers and educators.

Dr. David Olson from the University of Minnesota has discussed several. He observes, "One of the reasons that the marriage institution does not live up to its expectations is because of the many myths and unrealistic expectations that individuals bring to marriage." ("Marriage of the Future: Revolutionary or Evolutionary Change?" *The Family Coordinator* 12 [1972]: 385–86.) Dr. Olson then lists what he thinks are some common marriage myths:

Myth 1: If a sexual relationship is not good, it will spontaneously improve with time.

Myth 2: Marriage will always change or reform a person.

Myth 3: Marriage is easy; the difficulty is finding the right person.

Myth 4: Who you marry is more important than when you marry.

Myth 5: Your marriage partner will be able to satisfy all your needs.

Myth 6: The more time spent and activities shared together, the better the marriage relationship.

Myth 7: Patterns of behavior and interaction that develop in marriage are easy to change.

Myth 8: A quarrel or disagreement can only be detrimental to a marriage.

Myth 9: It is always best not to express negative feelings about one's spouse.

Myth 10: If a married couple loves each other, they will intuitively know what each other is feeling or wanting.

Myth 11: A good sexual relationship in marriage will be automatic and easy to develop.

Myth 12: If there is a good sexual relationship in marriage, other problems will take care of themselves.

Myth 13: Sexual adjustment in marriage will result more from proper techniques than from proper attitudes.

In 1990, Dr. Melvyn Kinder and Dr. Connell Cowan wrote in *Husbands and Wives: Exploding Marital Myths, Deepening Love and Desire* that one of the reasons half the married couples in the United States eventually divorce is because of what people initially or later come to expect from the marital relationship. In their chapter "Letting Go of Marital Myths," they write about how we come to believe myths and what some of those myths are:

> Most of us learn about marriage firsthand through an often frustrating, sometimes painful process of trial and error, occasionally hurting ourselves and our mates. We haven't been taught in any systematic fashion what we might expect or what might be expected of us. Instead, we pick up bits and pieces of information along the way from parents, early romantic adventures, and the media. Some of it is accurate and helpful, but unfortunately much of it is inaccurate and distorted. . . .
>
> You will notice that some of these myths are old and traditional in the sense that couples have always believed them to be true and they have always created dissention in marriage. A number of the other myths, however, are new, unfortunate by-products of the "me generation" and the excessive psychologizing of marriage to the point where anything seems possible and reasonable if only you just talk about it and negotiate it long enough. (New York: Penguin Books USA, Inc., 1990, pp. 30–32.)

Here, according to Dr. Kinder and Dr. Cowan, are some common current beliefs about marriage:

Myth 14: Marriage will always make you feel complete and whole.

Myth 15: Your mate should change for you if he or she really loves you.

Myth 16: If you truly love each other, romance should continue to flourish.

Myth 17: Differences in need should always be negotiated.

Myth 18: In a good marriage, the partners always have identical dreams and goals.

Myth 19: The more open you are with your mate, the more satisfying the marriage.

Myth 20: Sexual disinterest is inevitable in marriage.

Myth 21: If you're not feeling fulfilled, your marriage must be at fault.

Myth 22: Being a full-time wife and mother is a waste of potential.

Myth 23: A woman or man can be devoted fully to work, family, and marriage.

Myth 24: If you have to "work" on a marriage, something is wrong.

The two California marriage counselors concluded, "Those who cling tenaciously to these myths fail to understand a fundamental truth about change in marriage: there must be a void created for any new patterns to be established. And releasing one's mate from the burden of having to meet unrealistic expectations allows him or her to perceive you in a new way and to think about being different on his or her own terms." (P. 73.)

In their book written especially for newlyweds, Kathleen and Thomas Hart also have a chapter on expectations. In *The First Two Years of Marriage: Foundation for a Life Together*, they note:

> Probably most couples expect more of marriage than it can deliver, and have to undergo a painful disillusionment. We need our dreams, or

we might settle for less than we could have. But in the area of romantic love especially, an unreality can creep into our dreaming, setting us up for acute disappointment. . . . All of us want more intensity and excitement in life, and more love. . . . Perhaps if we look at some of the most common unrealistic expectations for marriage, and revise them, we will feel better about what we actually have in marriage and see more possibilities in it. (New York/Ramsey, New Jersey: Paulist Press, 1983, p. 7.)

According to the Harts, here are some additional marriage myths:
Myth 25: We will do everything together.
Myth 26: We will always feel the same way about things.
Myth 27: You will always be intensely interested in me, and I in you.
Myth 28: There will be a lot of sex and warm physical closeness.
Myth 29: You will meet all my deeper needs, and I yours.
Myth 30: The character defects I now see in you will disappear under the influence of my love.
Myth 31: The details of our living will fall naturally into place.
Myth 32: We will probably never fight.
Myth 33: We enter this marriage with pretty much the same expectations.
Myth 34: Our marriage will be different from all the bad ones we have seen. (See pp. 7–12.)

As newlyweds, you and your spouse may enter marriage with some unrealistic views of what it may be like. Since every marriage is a unique blend of two individuals, this uniqueness consequently creates marriages that are all different in some way. In spite of the differences, most young couples want some things in common, such as feeling both vulnerable and comfortable at the same time, respecting oneself and one's partner, having a healthy and

33

satisfying sexual relationship, desiring to help and support each other, and enhancing the ability to grow together.

Like the canoe-trip analogy in the introduction, life will sometimes present challenges that have no apparent solutions or answers. Even so, our marital relationship will grow and develop with time, if you work toward your common goals one day at a time. The unity in your marriage will strengthen as you balance your own attitudes, needs, and priorities against those of the husband or wife you have recently married.

To live with or reconcile differences in your marriage, you need to ask yourself, What are my expectations of marriage and my marriage partner? Are they realistic? Are they excessively high? Are they too low? How do my expectations compare with those of my marriage partner? Much of a couple's happiness in marriage depends on the expectations of both.

Most of the newlyweds I teach at Brigham Young University seem to be functioning quite well . . . above average, if there is such a measurement. But numerous newlyweds at BYU and elsewhere in the Church seem to be unhappy or disenchanted because, I believe, they have excessive or unrealistic expectations of themselves, their marriage partners, and even the relationship of marriage right from the day of the wedding.

MORTAL ASPECTS OF AN ETERNAL RELATIONSHIP

Some Latter-day Saints may wonder if some couples put too much emphasis on mortality and thereby ignore the eternal nature of marriage. Maybe so. Perhaps in some cases the opposite may also be true. We may put so much emphasis on eternity that we ignore the realities of mortal life. When we marry in the temple, we marry for both *time* (this life) and *eternity* (the next life). If we don't make it through mortality together in marriage, is there any guarantee that our relationships will continue in the eternities? Someone once said that we should not become so heavenly minded that we are of no earthly good.

Susan and I, along with all other Latter-day Saints, cherish the concept that the marital relationship can continue in the next life. (See D&C 132:19.) It is one of the most endearing and appealing aspects of the restored gospel of Jesus Christ. But we also know that we must make it through mortality in order to enjoy the blessings of eternity. That is the challenge for all.

I have often wondered if our concepts of eternity and perfection in some ways inhibit marriage during mortality. Do we expect too much too soon from our marriages, our spouses, and ourselves? Do we give up too soon? Do we marry too young? Do we inadequately prepare for marriage? Do we do too much comparing with others? Do we want instant perfection and lack the patience to strive for perfection over an entire lifetime?

We would do well to remember the insight that "we are not mortal beings having spiritual experiences, but spiritual beings having mortal experiences." As such, we should allow more time for ourselves and our spouses to develop and mature during our marriages. Maybe we need to go back to the basics and start practicing the first quality of love mentioned by both Paul and Mormon. It simply is "charity suffereth long." (1 Cor. 13:4; Moro. 7:45.)

. . . .

CHAPTER 5

SURVIVING THE FIRST YEAR

From my first month of marriage, I would like to share with newlyweds an incident that illustrates the fragile nature of wedded bliss. The first three weeks were nothing short of bubbly happiness. Susan and I got along just fine. Just like in the movies, or so we thought.

The last Saturday of that first month proved to be an interesting day . . . and evening. My parents were coming to our apartment for breakfast on their way through town, so we got up early to prepare the meal. My first mistake that day was not being very sensitive about my new bride's anxiety in fixing her first meal for her in-laws. My dad is somewhat of an expert when it comes to frying eggs, but we thought we could do well enough to pass inspection.

THE BROKEN EGG YOLK

About 9:00 A.M. our phone rang. My dad was calling from a local gas station. He said they had just arrived and would be to our apartment in about ten minutes. I hung up the phone and told Susan that my folks were on their way. She put the frying pan on the stove, warmed it up, put in a little butter, cracked an egg, and dropped it in the frying pan. But when the egg hit the frying pan, she started to cry.

I asked her why she was crying, and Susan replied, "The yolk broke!" I can't remember the exact words I said, but it was something like "A broken egg yolk isn't worth crying over." Whatever I said was not the right thing to say at the moment. Susan bristled and cried even harder. She said she simply wanted the fried eggs to be "just right" for my parents, and now, of all things, the yolk had broken on one of the eggs.

In hindsight, I should have been more sensitive to her feelings about wanting to make a good breakfast for my parents. But I mumbled something about bawling over broken egg yolks and not understanding what all the fuss was about. Susan got upset that I couldn't understand her feelings. I got even more upset about her getting more upset—all over a broken egg yolk.

A few minutes later, right on schedule, my folks arrived, and my wife and I temporarily set aside our egg yolk/crying discussion long enough to fry some new eggs, fix the rest of the breakfast, and spend a pleasant hour visiting with them before they left to continue their trip. Later that morning I asked Susan if we could talk about the broken-egg-yolk incident that happened earlier. That was a mistake. We talked and talked, and the discussion got deeper and deeper. For nearly one month of marriage, whatever feelings we had of dissatisfaction or discontentment with each other or our marriage had been held back or concealed. But when they came out, they came out all at once.

What happened that Saturday afternoon was that our bubble burst. By evening the broken egg yolk had been long forgotten. We allowed ourselves to go on and on, talking about what now seem like minor and trivial dissatisfactions. By eleven o'clock, we were asking questions like "Should we have really married each other?" and "Was our marriage prematurely doomed for failure?" and "Are we really going to make it in marriage?"

The next morning we went to Church. We were still downcast. Our plight was not helped when, in fast-and-testimony meeting, an elderly gentleman stood up and said he and his wife had been married for nearly fifty years and had "never had an argument." That was hard for us to take. They had gone for nearly fifty years (supposedly) without any argument or misunderstandings, and we had been able to make it only three weeks! We felt awful as we left church. We didn't think our marriage had a chance.

My sister, Jane, called on the phone that afternoon to chat for a few moments and see how we were doing. She and her husband, Lee, had been married for six years. I tried to conceal my hurts, but Jane could tell something was wrong. Finally I asked, "Jane, have you and Lee ever had an argument or disagreement?" "Of course we have," she assured me. I then related what the elderly church member had said. Jane told me that (1) the old gentleman was probably lying; (2) if not lying, he was probably forgetful; and (3) even if it were true, they would have had fifty years of a terribly boring and uneventful marriage.

Believing that there was still hope for our marriage, Susan and I began talking more that afternoon. I finally admitted that I should have been more sensitive to her feelings, and she finally admitted that a broken egg yolk just may be a questionable reason for crying. By nightfall, the incident was mostly behind us, and we recommitted ourselves to each other and our relationship.

Looking back at the incident, we now think it was rather humorous. I have told it often to singles and newlyweds because I think there is a lesson to be learned. Things that are terribly upsetting to us at the moment can later be recalled and even laughed at with a certain amount of levity.

In other ways, the incident was rather scary. Newlyweds of less than one month, we allowed ourselves to have a serious discussion on whether "we were meant for each other."

Every newly married couple will likely have their own egg-yolk incident. Such incidents take us through a transition from the ideal, the life of fantasy and make-believe, into the world of reality. Susan and I advise newly married couples not to take these first few incidents too seriously. It is like jerking a seedling out of the ground to see if the roots have begun to grow. What little plants need is nurturance for growth. Fortunately, Susan and I made the transition successfully during the weeks that followed.

SURVIVING THE FIRST YEAR OF MARRIAGE

A former student at BYU stopped by my office not long ago. He said he had been married a few weeks and was a little apprehensive. "I've got a few minutes before my next class," he said, "so tell me how to survive the first year of marriage." I had heard of short-term counseling, but this seemed to be a little extreme.

I said I didn't have a magic list of what "to do," but I did have four suggestions of what "not to do" during the first year of marriage.

1. *Don't Try Too Hard.* The first thing I suggested was not to try too hard at the beginning of marriage. This may seem like unusual advice since many divorces occur during the first year or two of marriage. But I have observed that many young couples divorce, not because they don't care, but because they often try to live their entire married life during the first year.

Those who marry in the '90s may not be aware that they have a good chance of celebrating a golden wedding anniversary if they just make it through the first few years. This period is merely the beginning — the starting blocks. I suggested that the student and his new wife just get to know each other better during the first year of marriage. Allow a year or two to establish a track record before making any judgments about the relationship.

I recalled a family friend many years ago who used a fine team of horses on his farm. He continuously admonished his farm hands not to work a good team to death. We frequently do that with marriage, overworking it without letting the relationship "rest." Marriage has the potential to be a fulfilling, satisfying relationship. But if excessive expectations are placed upon it, marriage, like the team of fine horses, becomes overburdened.

2. *Don't Try to Be Married Like Everyone Else.* Many newlyweds are confused because they don't know how married couples are supposed to act or interact. Frequently we want to be married like our parents, not realizing that they have had twenty years or more of experience. If only we could go back with our parents to their first few years of married life, we would have an entirely different perspective.

If not our parents' marriage, we try to emulate other older couples, such as married brothers or sisters and their spouses, aunts and uncles, neighbors and their spouses, or perhaps religious leaders and their partners. I suggested to the young man that he allow their own marital life-style to emerge without trying to make it like someone else's, or more important, like everyone else's.

3. *Don't Take Minor Incidents Too Seriously.* I briefly told my former student about the broken egg yolk and our overreaction. A word has been coined to describe what happened to us that day: *horribilizing.* We horribilize many events in life, which means we allow minor events to became major, monstrous ones. These incidents have elsewhere been termed "tremendous trifles." Such events are "tremendous" in that they are of major significance to one person but a mere "trifle" to another. Tremendous trifles include where we squeeze the toothpaste tube, where dirty socks and underwear belong, how one eats fried chicken, whether a marriage partner should sprawl or snuggle while sleeping (between snores), and what a man's razors can be used for in addition to shaving his face. These things, like broken egg yolks, should be dealt with but not blown out of proportion in marriage.

4. *Don't Be Too Rigid.* I finally cautioned the recently married student not to be too rigid in marriage at the beginning. Many times young husbands

and wives begin married life with rigid expectations for both themselves and their spouses. Though the expectations are derived from a variety of sources, they nonetheless emerge as fixed ideas. "You must do this! I must do that!"

There are at least three reasons why spouses must continuously adapt in marriage: (1) Some things about spouses can be known only after marriage. During courtship, individuals may hide part of themselves, or some may not be as perceptive as they should because of the romantic and physical attraction of the engagement period. But after marriage, the facades come down, and partners become known for what they are. (2) Many aspects of married life are difficult to anticipate or understand until they are experienced. Such things as mutual money management, in-laws, and idiosyncrasies of habit must be reconciled accordingly. (3) Individuals will change during marriage. Few people remain exactly as they are when they marry, even though their spouses may try to hold them to the behavior and personality characteristics that were initially attractive. This individual change requires the partner to adapt.

The bell rang, and my young friend thanked me for the quick advice and left. Such is short-term counseling. After a few minutes, I glanced up at the bulletin board above my desk. There was a three-step strategy for surviving married life if all else fails:

Step 1: Go around your house, gather up all the glass marbles, and put them in a jar.

Step 2: Every time your husband or wife does something to upset or annoy you, go to the jar, get a marble, and throw it out the window.

Step 3: Follow this sequence until all the marbles are gone.

Theory: Once you have lost all your marbles, your husband or wife won't bother you anymore.

Perhaps I should have given my former student that list as well.

FENCES OR AMBULANCES?

What could you do right at the beginning of your marriage to help you and your spouse stay in love and help prevent problems? You might start by building a few fences.

During a recent Education Week at BYU, I suggested that every LDS couple and family should take greater precautions in preventing marriage and family problems from happening. I then quoted a poem titled "A Fence or an Ambulance," based on the adage "An ounce of prevention is better than a pound of cure." It was written by an Englishman, Joseph Malins, several years ago.

'Twas a dangerous cliff, as they freely confessed,
Though to walk near its crest was so pleasant;
But over its terrible edge there had slipped
A duke and full many a peasant.
So the people said something would have to be done,
But their projects did not at all tally;
Some said, "Put a fence around the edge of the cliff,"
Some, "An ambulance down in the valley."

But the cry for the ambulance carried the day,
For it spread through the neighboring city;
A fence may be useful or not, it is true,
But each heart became brimful of pity
For those who slipped over that dangerous cliff;
And the dwellers in highway and alley
Gave pounds or gave pence, not to put up a fence,
But an ambulance down in the valley.

"For the cliff is all right, if you're careful," they said,

"And, if folks even slip or are dropping,
It isn't the slipping that hurts them so much,
As the shock down below when they're stopping."
So day after day, as these mishaps occurred,
Quick forth would these rescuers sally
To pick up the victims who fell off the cliff,
With their ambulance down in the valley.

Then an old sage remarked: "It's a marvel to me
That people give far more attention
To repairing results than to stopping the cause,
When they'd much better aim at prevention.
Let us stop at its source all this mischief," cried he,
"Come, neighbors and friends, let us rally;
If the cliff we will fence we might almost dispense
With the ambulance down in the valley."

"Oh, he's a fanatic," the others rejoined,
"Dispense with the ambulance? Never!
He'd dispense with all charities, too, if he could;
No! No! We'll support them forever.
Aren't we picking up folks just as fast as they fall?
And shall this man dictate to us? Shall he?
Why should people of sense stop to put up a fence,
While the ambulance works in the valley?"

But a sensible few, who are practical too,
Will not bear with such nonsense much longer;
They believe that prevention is better than cure,
And their party will soon be the stronger.
Encourage them then, with your purse, voice, and pen,
And while other philanthropists dally,

43

They will scorn all pretense and put up a stout fence
On a cliff that hangs over the valley.

Better guide well the young than reclaim them when old,
For the voice of true wisdom is calling,
"To rescue the fallen is good, but 'tis best
To prevent other people from falling."
Better close up the source of temptation and crime
Than deliver from dungeon and galley;
Better put a strong fence round the top of the cliff
Than an ambulance down in the valley.

(The Best Loved Poems of the American People
[New York: Doubleday, 1936], pp. 273–74.)

Many government, educational, and religious programs attempt to assist married couples and family members. The majority of these programs, however, focus on "cure" rather than "prevention." Though the medical profession has made great progress in the past four decades with preventing disease, organizations concerned with marriage and family have made limited progress in prevention, and that only in the past decade. The need for ambulances remains strong in our society. But one wonders if we could not reduce the fleet if more fences — better or more preventive measures — were installed.

We can move more quickly, however, in putting up personal fences than societal ones. We can look at ourselves and our marriages and put up railings around the danger areas. Don't let ourselves get too close to the cliff of immorality, for instance, by putting up fences that keep us from the questionable hype of media. Don't let us fall into the pit of greed by installing guard rails around the use of our money. The easiest problems to solve are the ones that don't happen.

CHAPTER 6

SEX AND INTIMACY

One aspect of marriage that most newlyweds look forward to is sexual intimacy. While sexual relations are often enjoyable and pleasurable in marriage, they can, in some circumstances, become frustrating and even disappointing. How can we keep sexual intimacy positive?

You have undoubtedly heard the old cliché "What you don't know can't hurt you." Not only is it a cliché, but also it is not true concerning sexual matters in marriage. What you don't know about sex and intimacy can hurt a great deal and cause much unnecessary pain in a relationship.

Several years ago Elder Hugh B. Brown noted the following about newlyweds in his book *You and Your Marriage* (Salt Lake City: Bookcraft, 1960): "Sex is not an unmentionable human misfortune, and certainly it should not be regarded as a sordid but necessary part of marriage. There is no excuse for approaching this most intimate relationship in life without true knowledge of its meaning and its high purpose. This is an urge which more insistently than others calls for self-control and intelligence." (P. 76.)

The LDS leader also noted, "Thousands of young people come to the marriage altar almost illiterate insofar as this basic and fundamental function is concerned. The sex instinct is not something which we need to fear or be ashamed of. It is God-given and has a high and holy purpose." (P. 73.)

The problem still exists for newlyweds entering the 1990s. This "illiteracy," though, now includes not only what they don't know, but also what they have learned or come to believe through the various forms of media. What faces young couples today is the overemphasis on sex in relationships. The steamy sex implied or depicted in movies, television, videos, or reading materials has created a distorted perspective of sexuality.

Some young couples may have heard the "beans in the bottle" theory of sexual frequency in marriage. Each time a couple have a sexual relationship during the first year of marriage, they put a bean in a bottle. Every time they have a sexual relationship after the first year, they take a bean out of the bottle. The theory? They will never completely empty the bottle. This story illustrates the myth of frequent and often uninhibited sexual relationships in the first year of marriage followed by a decrease in both intensity and frequency in the years that follow. During the first year of marriage, many couples may be on an unrealistic sexual treadmill, trying to keep up with the expectations that they have naïvely and unnecessarily imposed upon themselves.

If newlyweds don't feel the earth move or hear soul-stirring anthems during their first few sexual encounters, they may feel that something is wrong. Or, if the sexual passion lessens somewhat (down to normal) after a few months of marriage, they may likewise think their marriage is off to a bad start.

In addition to this, there are the notorious frequency counts: "Newlyweds, on the average, have sex _____ times per week" (fill in the blank). Is it once? Is it seven times? ten times? 2.4? 6.3? Is a marriage doomed if the couple are not "keeping up" with the supposed norm for the nation?

Newlyweds often ask, "How often is normal?" That is a good question. But what is "normal" for one couple may not be "normal" for another. (The frequencies, by the way, vary from several times a night to once every four to six weeks. Not surprisingly, most couples fall somewhere between those two parameters.)

The truth is that the frequency does not matter. The expected frequency is what causes the problems. If one person expects sexual relations several times a week, but they occur only once, that person will be frustrated or will think him- or herself unfulfilled. Another person may expect sexual relations only once a month but may experience them every other week. The first person has a sexual frequency of once a week and is unhappy. The second person has a sexual frequency of every other week and is happy. Why? The expected frequency is what contributes to the sexual fulfillment of a married couple.

Suppose a young married couple desires to improve the sexual relationship. Gender studies have shown that there is a noticeable difference between men and women. Improvement to the husband typically means more often. To the wife, improvement means better relationships. Men often keep frequency counts of the sexual encounters in marriage. "It's been _____ days/weeks now since we made love" might be a common complaint. Most wives often care little about frequency if fulfillment is not attained. The key is to help each other attain satisfaction during sexual relations. If couples focused more on sexual interests and likes, most relationships would dramatically improve.

The truth also is that spouses will not attain fulfillment each time they have sexual relations. An 80/20 ratio might be a good guide to follow. If the degree of sexual fulfillment is attained 80 percent of the time an attempt is made by husband and wife, then the relationship is successful. Perhaps 20 percent of the time, however, the husband or wife, for a variety of reasons, does not attain sexual fulfillment. When this occurs, it does not mean that something is wrong with the relationship. With a little sensitivity, the couple can remain intimate in other ways for an hour or two and then make another attempt. Couples willing to do so often find their efforts successful the second time.

The tradition and stereotype from the past are that husbands desire sex more frequently than wives. In September 1986, my article on intimacy, "They

Twain Shall Be One," appeared in the *Ensign*. The article brought in several letters, some of which took issue with one statement I made in the article. I noted, "Recent research indicates that the capacity for sexual response in women is just as great, and in some cases even greater, than that of males." (P. 51.) Many wrote to me and questioned the statement. It actually was a finding of William H. Masters and Virginia E. Johnson, who reported in *Human Sexual Response* (Boston: Little, Brown and Company, 1966) that we have underestimated and in many ways misunderstood female sexuality up until the recent past.

Men are often quite similar in their sexual responses. What stimulates one man will often stimulate others. And what stimulates a man on one occasion will usually stimulate him on another. Women, however, are more idiosyncratic or individualistic in their response to sexual stimuli. What stimulates one woman may not necessarily stimulate another woman. And what stimulates a woman on one occasion may not necessarily stimulate her on another.

Masters and Johnson reported that both males and females go through the same four phases of erotic response: excitement, plateau, orgasm, and resolution. (The last two phases may sometimes not be completed during sexual relations.) The orgasmic experience of women is similar to that of men except that there is no ejaculation. And women vary in the resolution stage. The capacity of women to respond to sexual stimuli is great in that they have the capacity to respond with several orgasms within just a few minutes. Men, however, can experience only one orgasm at a time with a varying refractory period (time between orgasms) of twenty to sixty minutes depending on the age and general health of the male at the time.

Let's see if the following diagrams will help us understand some of the differences in male/female sexual response. The sexual response in men has been noted to be fairly strong and constant. The response might look something like this:

The sexual response in women has been noted to be quite erratic but, on occasion, intense. The sexual response of women might look like this:

Superimposed on each other the diagrams illustrate the difference in sexual arousal in men and women:

Why there is such variation in a woman's sexual interest is not entirely known. Hormonal shifts involving estrogen account for some of it, as do emotional shifts and stresses in her day-to-day activities. But notice that, according to Masters and Johnson, women have a great, and sometimes greater, capacity for sexual response than do men.

Some time after the wedding, the state of arousal for a couple diminishes, and much of the time one will be sexually aroused when the other isn't. There are ways to resolve this by examining and renewing the dating and engagement period of the relationship. During engagement, couples spend a great deal of time talking to each other, touching each other, and generally building the relationship. It may be a matter of getting away from old stimuli and creating new ones. Simply going away together for a few days to a new location can help a couple rekindle the flame, if touch and talk are also present during the time together.

Dr. Lynn Scoresby once visited one of my classes for newlyweds at BYU as a guest lecturer on sexual relationships in marriage. One student asked him if there were any true aphrodisiacs (something that arouses sexual interest). He said, "Yes, prolonged conversation." He said that simple conversation between husband and wife for an extended period of time literally puts them in sync with each other and prepares them for more intimate interaction.

INTENDED FOR PLEASURE

Several years ago Dr. Ed Wheat, a Christian leader, and his wife, Gaye Wheat, wrote a book, *Intended for Pleasure* (Old Tappan, New Jersey: Fleming H. Revell Co., 1977), that was somewhat controversial at the time. In the book, the Wheats stated their belief that the sexual relationship in marriage was created by deity with the intent of giving intense pleasure for both husbands and wives in marriage. They wrote that since God created both male and female (see Gen. 1:27), much of the way we respond to sexual stimuli is innate and subsequently God-given. (See p. 17.)

Not all we feel or know about sexual matters may be innate. But for the vast majority, sex is an instinct present in almost all men and women, whether or not they have learned anything about it. And the fact that sexual intimacy can generate such an intense pleasurable response makes one wonder, Who devised all this and created in us the capacity to respond accordingly?

During the years I have taught at BYU, many newly wedded wives have come to me for private consultation. Some have confided in me their frustration and disappointment with the sexual aspect of their first few months of marriage.

Invariably a few report little or no sexual satisfaction in the relationship. In those cases, I show them the Wheats' book. I ask them if they believe that sexual relationships are intended for joy and pleasure. Surprisingly enough, the answer often is "no." After they read Genesis 1:27, I ask them if they believe that God created the human bodies, *both* male and female. At that point I discuss with them the female organ known as the clitoris. Some young women I have talked to have never heard about it or do not know where it is located. It is one of the little organs noted in Ed Wheat's book that God created in the female and that has no reproductive function whatsoever. It is there for one purpose only: to produce pleasure.

Because the male genitalia is external, there is little difficulty in either stimulation or subsequent satisfaction. The clitoris in the female, however, is smaller and somewhat concealed. It is therefore more difficult to locate and more difficult to stimulate. For many females, however, stimulation of the clitoris is a major source of sexual satisfaction, and couples should be aware of this.

THE SEXUAL RELATIONSHIP IS ONLY PART OF MARRIAGE

The sexual part of the marriage can be one of genuine excitement, intrigue, and fulfillment. But one point that many couples do not realize is this: *The sexual aspect of a marriage is an extension of the relationship and not the relationship itself.*

Many married couples, both young and old, believe that the sexual relationship in marriage is a good measure of the overall health of a marriage. If the sexual relationship is good, the marriage must be good. Conversely, if the sexual relationship is bad, then the marriage must be in trouble. This is not only an erroneous but also a dangerous belief on which to begin a marriage.

There are many happily married couples, some of whom are newlyweds, who have sexual problems, adjustments, or even dysfunctions.

Young LDS couples who obey the law of chastity during courtship reap one of the benefits of that commandment: they establish a fulfilling relationship prior to marriage without sexual involvement with each other. While sexual intimacy is usually something they desire, they have built a relationship that is not subject to the whims of sexual passion. The admonition from Alma is still relevant today: "Bridle all your passions, that ye may be filled with love." (Alma 38:12.)

One of the most sobering accounts of a sexual relationship before marriage is found in the Old Testament, in 2 Samuel 13:1–15. It is about Amnon, who loved Tamar so much he was "vexed" and "fell sick." Tamar was a virgin, and "Amnon thought it hard for him to do any thing [sexually] to her." (V. 2.) But his cunning friend Jonadab told him of a scheme whereby he might pursue some of his lustful desires toward Tamar. Jonadab suggested that Amnon pretend he was sick and request that Tamar bring some food to him in his bedroom. When they were alone, he would have the chance to act on his baser passions.

Amnon lay down "and made himself sick" (v. 6), then asked that Tamar might prepare some food and bring it to him. When Tamar came with the food, Amnon had all the men and women sent out of his house. Next, he invited Tamar into his chambers (bedroom). Then, "he took hold of her, and said unto her, Come lie with me." (V. 11.)

Tamar protested. "Nay, my brother, do not force me; for no such thing ought to be done in Israel: do not thou this folly. And I, whither, shall I cause my shame to go? and as for thee, thou shalt be as one of the fools in Israel." (Vv. 12–13.) Tamar then suggested that Amnon ask King David for her hand in marriage.

But Amnon couldn't wait: "Howbeit he would not hearken unto her voice; but, being stronger than she, forced her, and lay with her." (V. 14.)

Note what happened. What Amnon thought was love was little more than sexual passion. What he believed was love was only lust. His body had overpowered his brain. He was not in love, he was in heat! What happened immediately after the sexual act was completed? "Then Amnon hated her exceedingly; so that the hatred wherewith he hated her was greater than the love wherewith he had loved her. And Amnon said unto her, Arise, be gone." (V. 15.)

Unfortunately, the story of Amnon and Tamar has been enacted numerous times by young couples, both in and out of the Church. When the relationship is based on little more than idyllic romance and sexual passion, the relationship is almost always doomed from the beginning. As a test for engaged couples, I ask them to momentarily set aside passion and romance. What is left? Often young couples will realize how shallow their relationships really are. The reality is that someone can be romantically and sexually attracted to another person whom they don't even like, let alone know. Sex can never be a successful foundation for marriage.

Not long ago, a young woman in her middle twenties related to me the background behind her divorce. She thought that she was in love with a young man, and he with her. They were highly attracted to each other sexually and had approached the limits of inappropriate behavior several times during their dating and engagement. They even fantasized together what the sexual relationship would be like after marriage. They had failed to follow the admonition of Alma about bridling passions so that they might be filled with love. (See Alma 38:12.)

The night of their wedding, however, they had an Amnon-and-Tamar experience. After the overanticipated sexual relationship had been experi-

53

enced, they were both disappointed. In fact, that very night the young husband told his new bride that he really didn't know how much he loved her. Within a few days he left her, and before a month had passed, he had applied for a divorce. Why was a bride of only one week a divorced woman a few months later? We both concluded that the overemphasis on sex had distorted the relationship and kept them from exploring other, more enduring dimensions of the relationship.

SPOUSES AND SEXUAL FULFILLMENT

Many women, young and old, have been taught or believe that sex is all a man ever wants in marriage. When I was writing the book *What Husbands Expect of Wives,* one of my neighbor friends, a woman, suggested I would have to write only one chapter! We can joke all we want. The truth is that most husbands place great significance on sexual relations as a way to both give and receive love. I have said in many seminars that women can do everything else to try to convey that they love their husbands, but if they neglect the sexual aspect of marriage, their husbands will not know that they are loved, nor will they be able to express their love fully.

Such a comment is not original with me. Dr. Marian Hillard, an obstetrician, gynecologist, and woman, gives this advice to her female patients:

> The way to save a strained marriage . . . is to start with the act of love [meaning sexual intercourse]. Here are the essentials of marriage in concentrated form. In one act are consideration, warmth, gaiety, charm, hunger and ecstasy. In this small kingdom, a woman can heal the wounds caused by indifference and contempt. She is a fool, if she ignores this tool provided her by nature. . . . If women spent half the time cultivating the sexual relationship that they sometimes spend avoiding it, their marriages should blossom. (As quoted in Mike and Joyce Grace, *A Joyful Meeting:*

Sexuality in Marriage [St. Paul, Minnesota: International Marriage Encounter, Inc., 1980), p. 74.)

A young wife once asked me in a counseling session, "Should I give my husband sex even when I don't feel I should?" The question was loaded, asked with overtones of irritation and contempt. I first suggested that sex should not be some commodity that is exchanged for something else in marriage. Unfortunately, many people still think that "sex is something women give to get love, and love is something men give to get sex."

The young woman was disturbed by her husband's seemingly cavalier attitude toward sex and his apparent indifference to her feelings about it. "Even after we have had a fight or haven't gotten along for some time, he gets frisky and tries to get me into the bed. How can he even attempt sex when the feelings are frayed?" she asked.

It has become obvious to me over the years that sex is highly symbolic to both men and women. Many individuals attach differing meanings to it in different situations. I suggested to the young wife that men often see sex as a way to mend hurt feelings and wounds. On the other hand, women view sex as a sign, or symbol, that the hurts and wounds have been healed.

One can understand, therefore, the frustration of the young wife, who thought her husband insensitive to her feelings when he tried to be sexually intimate. He, however, rather than being totally inept and insensitive, believed that sexual relationships were a way to accomplish the very thing she wanted — to mend feelings and heal raw emotions. By becoming more sensitive to each other's perception of sex, both husband and wife could understand the other's symbolic attachment to sexual matters.

Sexual matters in marriage have a variety of meanings and purposes. For many couples, sex is one way of erotic response — "intended for pleasure." For others, it is simply a way to relax and release tension. Still for others, sex does not release tension but produces it, depending on the big three Ms: (1) mood, (2) moment, and (3) method. A few have suggested that sexual relations have religious connotations, becoming a marital sacrament, with the bed a symbolic altar. And obviously, a few couples still perceive that the only legitimate purpose of sex is impregnation and creation of children.

It is no mystery to many marriage counselors and educators that couples have so many problems with sex because of the many differing meanings and perceptions they attach to it. We have become so analytical that we suffer "analysis paralysis."

I believe that sex was created for a variety of reasons, one of which was as a natural way for husbands and wives to convey love, care, and sensitivity. Most books, however, on sexuality in marriage are either so blatant that they are offensive or so bland that they are not helpful. Not long ago, I received a copy of a book titled *The Marriage Bed: Renewing Love, Friendship, Trust and Romance* (Seattle: Madrona Publishers, 1986). The authors, William M. Womack, M.D., and Fred F. Strauss, seem to have struck somewhat of a balance.

According to the preface, *The Marriage Bed* is a prescription for marital health and emotional well-being. The basic premises of the book are that enduring passion results from a combination of love, friendship, trust, and romance, and that if sexual passion can endure, the likelihood of a rich, satisfying, and lasting marriage is much greater. The authors note:

> Sex is undeniably a big part of every marriage. Whether a couple talks about it or ignores it, their sex life greatly influences how they feel about themselves, each other and their marriage. A gratifying sex life not only makes marriage better, but makes all of life better. Satisfying sex leads to a greater appreciation of sex itself, one's partner and oneself. While a satisfying sexual relationship can't necessarily save a marriage, the absence of a satisfying sex life can certainly impair one.

The benefits of a satisfying married sex life are bountiful. In the first place, sex is pleasure. It's a great way to put aside the struggles of life for a while and simply feel good. When each partner feels self-confident in a sexual relationship, they each feel more confidence in their bodies and in life in general. This attitude, in turn, grows into a general increase in self-esteem. Sex also provides shared feelings—feelings that range from love, caring and closeness, to playfulness and fun. As this sharing grows, a special bond develops between the two lovers—a bond that strengthens the marriage. . . .

The key to a rich sex life is actually quite simple for most of us. Satisfying sex occurs when the partners have each learned to be comfortable with their own sexuality, their lover and the sexual situation. Instead of sexual performance being the primary focus, both partners learn to enjoy each moment of each sexual activity. As this happens, they both become more and more satisfied with the sexual relationship. Feelings grow deeper and desire occurs more frequently. . . .

As you improve your sex life, you will also improve the other parts of your marriage. Both of you will learn to express your feelings more easily and completely. This will help you . . . deal more quickly and easily with any conflicts that arise between you. You'll learn more about how to share love and pleasure. (Pp. 3–7.)

SUGGESTIONS FOR INTIMACY

Latter-day Saint newlyweds may be wise to make a commitment to each other for continued intimacy throughout the marriage. This includes but is not limited to sexual relationships. Such a commitment may be a key factor in staying married during the decades ahead.

President Spencer W. Kimball spent many hours counseling married couples during his years as a Church leader. He noted, "If you study the divorces [in the LDS Church], as we have had to do in these past years, you will find there are one, two, three, four reasons. Generally sex is the first. They did not get along sexually. They may not say that in the court. They may not even tell that to their attorneys, but that is the reason." (*Teachings of Spencer W. Kimball,* p. 312.)

To avoid this major contributing factor to marital disruption, married couples may find the following suggestions to be helpful:

1. Agree to talk often and openly about your sexual relationship. Seek to help each other attain intimacy in your marriage. If both of you are aware of the dynamics involved in giving and receiving, you will find that the more you give, the more you get is the general rule. Make a good sex life in your marriage a high priority for both of you.

2. Realize that intimacy can exist apart from sexual relationships, and seek intimacy in other ways such as communication, joint activities, and spiritual endeavors.

3. Take time, or arrange times, for intimacy and sexual fulfillment. This is critical in contemporary marriage because of more hectic schedules resulting, in part, from an increasing number of wives in the work force.

4. Read 1 Corinthians 7:2–5 often. What are the implications of verse five for newlyweds?

5. Focus on the total marital relationship. Remember that sex is an extension of the relationship and not the relationship itself. Work to improve other areas of your marriage along with the sexual dimension.

6. Remember the first two qualities of Christ-like love mentioned in the scriptures: "Charity suffereth long [is patient], and is kind." (1 Cor. 13:4; Moro. 7:45.) This is particularly true in the sexual relationships in marriage.

7. Understand that sex serves several functions in a marriage, including relationship enhancement, reproduction, personal fulfillment, communication, pleasure, spiritual development, and, on occasion, tension release.

8. Sexual fulfillment probably results from 90 percent attitude and 10 percent skills.

9. What we don't know can hurt us. Seek to eliminate misunderstandings about sex, especially those perpetuated by the media. When necessary, study and learn from appropriate sources about the sexual area of marriage.

10. Focus on your success in regard to your sexual relationship rather than on your failures. Remember that compliments bring far better results than complaints.

11. On occasion, allow for some variation, within propriety, in some aspects of your sexual relationship. Break the routines. Something as simple as changing time and place of sexual interaction can help greatly. Routine sexual relationships, with little or no variation in either circumstances or conditions, may be deadly to your relationship.

In an essay entitled "Intelligence and Affection," Elder Parley P. Pratt wrote the following more than a century ago:

> Some persons have supposed that our natural affections were the results of a fallen and corrupt nature, and that they are *"carnal, sensual, and devilish,"* and therefore ought to be resisted, subdued, or overcome as so many evils which prevent our perfection, or progress in the spiritual life. . . . Our natural affections are planted in us by the Spirit of God, for a wise purpose; and they are the very main-springs of life and happiness — they are the cement of all virtuous and heavenly society — they are the essence of charity, or love; and therefore never fail, but endure forever. There is not a more pure and holy principle in existence than the affection which glows in the bosom of a virtuous man for his companion. . . .
>
> The fact is, God made man, male and female; he planted in their bosoms those affections which are calculated to promote their happiness and union. That by that union they might fulfill the first and great commandment, . . . "To multiply and replenish the earth, and subdue it."

59

From this union of affection, springs all the other relationships, social joys and affections diffused through every branch of human existence. And were it not for this, earth would be a desert wild, an uncultivated wilderness. (*Writings of Parley Parker Pratt,* ed. and publ. Parker Pratt Robinson, [Salt Lake City, 1952], pp. 52–54.)

CHAPTER 7

MANAGING YOUR MONEY

A s a Latter-day Saint marriage counselor and educator, I am obviously interested in anything that disrupts marriages. As noted in the introduction, nearly two-thirds of couples who marry at the present time in the United States are expected to divorce. Whether LDS couples will participate in this trend to the same degree is not yet known. But I am convinced of one thing. How we as married couples manage our money has a great deal to do with marriage stability, for if we fail to learn how to manage our money, it surely will manage us!

How married couples earn and manage (or mismanage) their money is a major factor in marital stability or disruption. Wage earners spend an estimated 80 percent of their waking hours earning, spending, or worrying about money! Where we spend our money is also a good measurement of what we value in life. "For where your treasure is, there will your heart be also." (Matt. 6:21.) Not surprisingly, husbands and wives often value different things.

Money management requires communication, mutual decision making, and problem-solving skills. Unresolved financial problems and the subsequent frustration and anger can also be detrimental to the sexual relationship as well as to other areas of a marriage.

In the decade of the 1990s, we will face new situations and problems with money acquisition and money management: (1) With more than half of the wives in the U. S. gainfully employed, many couples now have access to a much larger income. (2) Due to extreme competition between lending companies, consumer credit is now much easier to obtain than in previous years. (3) As a result of increased income and easy-to-obtain credit, consumer debt is at an all-time high. (4) Bankruptcy is more common because of high debt and the inability to manage money. (5) With more disposable income, and more debt, financial get-rich-quick schemes seem to abound. Never has this proverb been truer: "A fool and his money are soon parted."

MONEY MANAGEMENT

Almost every poll or study done on problem areas in marriage indicates that money management is either number one or high on the list. Why is this so?

In the United States we are socialized to want to acquire things. This starts extremely early in childhood as we watch thousands of television commercials encouraging us to buy certain cereals and snacks, to obtain not only one but several toy vehicles and dolls. We supposedly will be unpopular if we do not purchase the right toothpaste or body deodorant or wear the most modern fashions in clothing. We consequently believe, or are led to believe, that we are not successfully married until we acquire certain things in life. If we are not cautious, we develop high expectations of what is essential in housing, transportation, furniture, appliances, tableware, and home entertainment. In acquiring these "necessities" of life, we often feel that just anything will not do. We want better things—better homes, better cars, better furniture, and better quality in everything we purchase.

There is nothing wrong in wanting excellent value for our dollars. But it isn't limited to just desiring excellent value. There is always more to acquire—a feeling that what we have is not sufficient because there is something "better." Furthermore, through a multibillion-dollar advertising industry, we are led to think that the things we own represent our position or station in life and even who we are. And the more we own, the higher our position and status supposedly are, and the more worthwhile we supposedly become.

We often build traps for ourselves in believing that the main measure of our self-worth is the extent to which we receive the esteem of others. Possessing a large sum of money or the things that it can buy may seem to bring the desired acceptance and esteem.

This quest to acquire things continues from childhood into our single years of adult life. Then we marry and find that the very nature of marriage sometimes drains off much of the money we would otherwise like to spend on ourselves. We invest heavily in homes, children, insurance, cars, education, and whatever is necessary to operate and maintain a home. Stress begins to mount over differences and disagreements on how the money should be spent. Couples often become easily offended and even outraged at the seemingly unwarranted expenditures of each other, and purchases that tax a couple's resources can impose unfair deprivations on a spouse.

Fights over money do not necessarily concern dollar bills. The problems that money creates in marriage can stem from the symbolic meaning that dollar bills represent to the individuals involved. The disagreement over money may actually be a disagreement about both the symbol and its worth in life.

The management of money, therefore, becomes a test of the couple's identity in marriage. It is a way to measure the "we feeling," the sense of togetherness couples establish through common goals and values. Problems may arise over the inability to talk about money or to decide jointly what "we" want to do with "our" money. This consensus is usually attained only when the couple can share their hopes and fears. They also eventually learn to show their trust and caring and to give each other understanding and support.

Only after they have learned to do these things can they wisely manage their money. This is because fights over money management usually are interpreted as "You don't trust me," "You don't understand me," or "You don't love me." Unfortunately, many couples faced with such problems proceed with divorce, the meaning and management of money being the root cause.

But other newlyweds are more fortunate. They realize that the financial situation they face in their marriage is *not* caused by their lack of love for each other. (They usually care deeply about each other!) They simply need some help in learning how to manage their money based on a philosophy where both share the responsibility for planning and both share the responsibility for the dispersement or allocation of resources. Therefore: *Money management is important in a marriage because of the symbols money represents and the differing values these symbols often have.* (See David R. Mace, "Areas of Adjustment in Marriage," in *Close Companions* [New York: Continuum Publishers Company, 1982], p. 113 for elaboration on the topic of money management in marriage.)

Having a successful marriage requires that a couple first agree on what they value, individually and jointly: How and where do we want to spend our money? The allocation of money is a fairly accurate measurement of what we value in life. Simply examining last year's canceled checks, for example, can give us some enlightening insights into what we have valued in the past.

The second requirement is that we participate in allocating our financial resources. This requires some planning and forethought before the money comes in, rather than jointly commiserating at the end of the month when the money is gone.

Most newlyweds should realize that more money will not solve their problems. We often assume that if we had just a few thousand dollars more each year, our financial troubles would vanish. Many are surprised to find that couples earning two hundred thousand dollars or more are sometimes among those who have the greatest money problems, simply because they haven't yet learned to manage their income. *No amount of money will suffice if husband*

and wife have an inadequate means of handling it. Successful couples of lesser means are those who have learned to manage what they do have — and they are much happier than those who have or earn vast amounts of money and yet are inept managers.

Another crucial concept to consider is this: *Expenditures always rise to meet the income.* This simply means that no matter how much you earn, you will always find something else to buy with the additional money. Because of the varied interests and wants of two individuals in a marriage, couples have no difficulty spending all the money that is available. Couples can even spend more than what they have through the credit so readily available today. At some point in the marriage, and it might as well be at the beginning, a husband and wife have to discuss and agree on what they will do with the money they have in their possession. For many couples today, that amount over a lifetime may well exceed a million dollars! If a couple married in their twenties and maintained an income of thirty thousand dollars for fifty years of marriage, they would have managed one million five hundred thousand dollars. Maybe the problem some couples have with money management today is not having too little, but actually having too much. This is the irony in the statement that "no married couple ever has enough money."

In the traditional marriages of the past, husbands earned almost all the money and frequently had the only say in where the money went or how it was spent. Many wives did not know how much money their husbands earned, nor were they aware how it was being spent. All they were aware of, if they had any involvement in family finances, was the amount given them each month for food, housekeeping, and perhaps personal use. There are situations today in which a husband dies, and the wife does not even know where the checkbook is kept or how to write a check if she does find it.

Today nearly 60 percent of wives are employed and earn nearly 25 percent of the family income. It is anticipated that, by the turn of the century, 80 percent of wives will be employed part- or full-time and earn 40 percent of the family money. With these trends in mind, husbands need to realize that contemporary wives should have more say in money management than in the past. Decades ago, families operated under a one-vote system, with the husband having the only vote. That philosophy will no longer work, and couples must carefully examine the decision-making structure in their marriages.

TWO CHECKBOOKS

Most married couples probably operate out of one checkbook managed by either the husband or wife. One manages the checking account because the other is disinterested or doesn't have the time to do it or because one happens to be better at budgeting than the other. According to some financial experts, however, there are several good reasons why husbands and wives should maintain individual checking accounts. (See James P. Christensen and Clint Combs with George Durrant, *Rich on Any Income: The Easy Budgeting System That Fits in Your Checkbook* [Salt Lake City: Shadow Mountain, 1987].) In this case, husbands and wives put their allocated monthly income into two separate checking accounts, and each spouse has a financial stewardship over his or her account. The amount of money and the type of expenses each is accountable for are negotiated each month. Here are four advantages of two checking accounts:

1. When both husband and wife have an individual checking account, it is a tangible symbol that both are sharing financial management practices. In addition, two checking accounts give them each a means whereby planning and spending can be done jointly.

2. Decision making has a certain amount of power associated with it, particularly with decisions made about money. When one or the other makes most or all the decisions in marriage, the relationship becomes lopsided. Money

management is but one way to balance decision making in a marital relationship so that both husband and wife participate.

3. Even though there is a small monthly charge for the second checkbook, checks, and service charge, the system "saves" in more important ways. It saves on emotions, frustration, frayed nerves, and stress. One does not have to ask the other for money. And a couple will enjoy greater peace of mind.

4. All family members — husband, wife, and children — need access to a certain amount of money that they can control. There is a psychological payoff when a person is in some degree of control of his or her life. When a person controls or handles the money for another, there is a psychological price that all involved must pay.

Any effort made to manage financial resources better will yield rich rewards in a marriage relationship. Couples who stabilize marriage through effective money management make giant strides toward successful marriages.

THE LORD'S TENTH

No matter how you choose to manage your money as newlyweds, no matter how much money you as a couple earn or how you manage it, I am sure of one thing. I do not believe you will prosper in either physical or spiritual matters if you do not learn and adhere to the concept of tithing, or paying one-tenth of your annual increase to the Lord.

As a result of the financial chaos that seems prevalent, LDS couples may, in fact, struggle more today with tithing and financial offerings than ever before. With the stress of high debts, Church members may feel that they "can't afford to pay tithing" at the very time they need to pay it the most. President Heber J. Grant said this about tithing:

> The law of financial prosperity to the Latter-day Saints, under covenant with God, is to be an honest tithepayer, and not to rob the Lord

in tithes and offerings. Prosperity comes to those who observe the law of tithing; and when I say prosperity I am not thinking of it in terms of dollars and cents alone, although as a rule the Latter-day Saints who are the best tithepayers are the most prosperous men, financially; but what I count as real prosperity, as the one thing of all others that is of great value to every man and woman living, is the growth in a knowledge of God, and in a testimony, and in the power to live the gospel and to inspire our families to do the same. That is prosperity of the truest kind. (Conference Report, April 4, 1925, p. 10.)

Many Latter-day Saints may pay tithing to avoid being burned at the Second Coming of the Lord (see D&C 64:23) or to avoid robbing God (see Mal. 3:8). While these are worthwhile motives, there are other, more positive motives for paying tithing. Tithing is the Lord's plan and base for family financial stability in this dispensation as in others. Following are two solid reasons that the Lord has given to keep his financial law:

1. *Tithing Is an Earthly Test.* Many passages in scripture teach that one of the reasons we came to this earth from the premortal state was to be tested. (See D&C 98:14; Abr. 3:25.) Paying our tithing is apparently a test whereby commitment and loyalty to the Lord and his kingdom might be determined. President Joseph F. Smith noted:

By this principle (tithing) the loyalty of the people of this Church shall be put to the test. By this principle it shall be known who is for the kingdom of God and who is against it. By this principle it shall be seen whose hearts are set on doing the will of God and keeping his commandments, thereby sanctifying the land of Zion unto God, and who are opposed to this principle and have cut themselves off from the blessings of Zion. There is a great deal of importance connected with this principle, for by it it shall be known whether we are faithful or unfaithful. In this respect it is as essential as faith in God, as repentance of sin, as baptism for the remission of sin, or as the laying on of hands for the gift of the Holy Ghost. . . . Tithing is a test by which the people as individuals shall be proved. Any man who fails to observe this principle shall be known as a man who is indifferent to the welfare of Zion, who neglects his duty as a member of the Church. . . . He neglects to do that which would entitle him to receive the blessings and ordinances of the gospel. (*Gospel Doctrine* [Salt Lake City: Deseret Book Company, 1977], pp. 225–26.)

Paying tithes and offerings identifies us as being for the kingdom of God. It involves us in "the welfare of Zion." And by keeping this commandment, we set in motion a process whereby the Lord can protect us from the destroyer. (See Mal. 3:10-11.)

2. *The Lord Asks for the First Fruits.* Susan and I had been married only five months when we discovered a major difference in our thinking. It had something to do with tithing. She had been taught when she was young that whenever she earned money, she should pay her tithing soon afterwards, the same week if possible. While growing up, I too believed and practiced the payment of tithing but I had a somewhat different approach. I believed that as long as I paid it annually, I had until midnight, December 31, to do so.

We received our first paycheck from my father shortly after we were married. At the time I was managing his service station in Centerfield, Utah. Susan was adamant that we pay tithing immediately. I countered that it really didn't matter as long as we paid it within the year. The discussion continued for several weeks with other paychecks.

A few months later we returned to BYU for my senior year of college. Susan had a job teaching first grade at Cherry Hill Elementary School in Orem. During November, some friends called and said they were going to purchase half a beef. They wanted to know if we wanted to buy the other half for $160.

(That was 1965!) We didn't have enough money right then outside of the tithing we were planning to pay that Sunday. I suggested to Susan that we buy the beef and pay double tithing the following month when I received my check from the National Guard. We discussed it back and forth for a few hours that night, and I finally persuaded her that we should buy the beef and postpone paying our tithing to the following month. So we took our tithing money and the additional amount we needed and bought the beef.

But do you think Susan would let me enjoy it during the months that followed? She would cook a roast or fry some steaks and then call, "Here, Brent, come and eat the Lord's beef!" Somehow I didn't enjoy it as much as I thought I would. She was correct in her assessment of paying tithing. If I had studied the scriptures carefully, I would have found earlier that she was right! In ancient times the Lord commanded the people to bring in the "firstfruits" of their labors and to give the "firstlings" of the flocks, which required great faith since neither the total harvest nor the increase in animals would be known at the time. (See Ex. 23:19; Lev. 23:10; 27:26; Mosiah 2:3.)

FINANCIAL OFFERINGS: A BLESSING OR BURDEN?

Just a few years later, Susan and I learned a valuable lesson about financial offerings to the Lord. I am thankful we learned it early in our marriage so the principle could help guide our lives as a couple.

We were graduate students at Florida State University, and I was serving as branch president for about forty undergraduate students. One evening the district and branch leaders met for a special meeting with President Malone Peddie, president of the Tallahassee, Florida, District. President Peddie reported that the Church was going to build a temple in Washington, D.C., and all Latter-day Saints in the eastern and southern part of the United States were invited to contribute. President Peddie asked if the student branch could donate one thousand dollars to the construction of the temple.

I hesitated before I gave my response, and when I did, I reminded President Peddie that the student branch had only forty members, most of whom were living on limited incomes. President Peddie still asked that we see what we could do.

To be honest, I didn't feel right about asking the small student branch to help raise one thousand dollars. Maybe two or three hundred but not one thousand. So at our next sacrament meeting, I told the students in the branch about the Washington, D.C., Temple and stated that their contributions to the construction of the temple would be welcomed. The branch presidency said nothing about the one thousand dollars we had been asked to raise.

The weeks went by, and we did raise about two hundred dollars. With just four weeks left, it didn't look like much more would be donated. Late one night I was in my office in the LDS chapel in Tallahassee. President Peddie was also there in his office. He stopped in to ask me, "Brent, how is the student branch doing on the money for the Washington Temple?"

Once again I reminded President Peddie of the student status of most of the branch. I said that I didn't feel comfortable asking them for more than the few hundred dollars they had contributed thus far. Then came the lesson.

"Brent," said President Peddie, "do you view financial offerings to the Lord as a burden or blessing?"

I hesitated to answer because I *had* truly perceived the contribution as a burden upon the students.

In his pleasant southern drawl, President Peddie said, "When you get to heaven, Brent, you may have to stand before the Lord and be accountable to him for withholding blessings to those in your branch."

"Withholding blessings? What do you mean?" I asked.

71

President Peddie explained that most people perceived financial offerings to the Lord as a burden. He reassured me that attendant blessings, both temporal and spiritual, come to those who make their financial offerings. He bid me good night and left.

I sat at my desk, dumbfounded. Was it possible that I was withholding blessings from those in my branch by not inviting them more earnestly to contribute to the building of the Washington, D. C., Temple?

The following Sunday I related the incident with President Peddie to the student branch. I told them for the first time of the one thousand dollars that was needed from our branch. I asked how many of them viewed financial offerings as a burden and shared with them President Peddie's testimony of the blessings that come to those who give.

We had only three weeks to go. I will never forget what happened. The students sacrificed and sold some of their books. Some went to work at part-time jobs to earn a few extra dollars to donate to the Washington, D.C., Temple fund. Others went without a few things that they had thought were necessities. During the following three weeks, the Tallahassee, Florida, student branch raised more than eight hundred dollars. There is no question that we would have raised the full amount had I learned earlier a simple but profound truth: Financial offerings to the Lord are truly a blessing . . . and not a burden.

Financial management for Latter-day Saints is based not only on principles of sound financial planning, but also on principles of righteousness. If we wish to invite the Lord to help us manage our money and alleviate our debts, we must keep our promises to him.

. . . .

CHAPTER 8

CONTINUING THE COMMUNICATION

You have likely learned as newlyweds to communicate fairly well on one particular matter: the decision to marry! Recall the many long discussions you had about the potential marriage. There may have been moments of indecision and differences of opinions, such as when and where to marry. Whom should you invite to the wedding? Who should be the best man? The bridesmaids? How did you decide on the honeymoon plans and the other associated details, all requiring considerable communication? You are to be congratulated on your ability to communicate on something very important. The challenge now comes for both of you to continue the communication patterns you have developed thus far. How can you continue to talk to each other, often for extended periods of time, on matters of mutual interest and concern? And in what ways can your communication as newlyweds be improved?

One of the statements often heard from married couples a few years after marriage is "We just can't communicate." But it is not a true statement. *It is impossible not to communicate.* What couples often mean is that they have difficulty communicating on certain matters or topics. The fact is, they may be communicating very well on less-troublesome aspects of their marriage. Many couples may find that they need some insights, skills, and encouragement on how to communicate more effectively on particular areas of mutual concern and interest.

If asked to describe important skills in effective communication, some would say, "Use eye-to-eye contact," "Be a good listener," "Send clear messages," "Don't interrupt the other when he or she is speaking," and so on. All of these are important. But in my opinion, the one most important skill in effective communication is caring. The simple truth is that people will usually try to communicate if they feel the other person cares about them. Therefore, if spouses feel no care or consideration from their partners, they will not communicate well, if at all, no matter how many of the other skills are acquired.

For a moment, think back on your own life. Who do you feel cared about you? It might have been your parents or brother or sister. It could have been a trusted friend, coach, or teacher. If you remember, you will recall many pleasant conversations that you had with these individuals without a lot of worry about "how to communicate." Because they cared, you probably talked — frequently and deeply — on topics of mutual concern and interest.

Learning to care about another individual — and effectively conveying that care — is probably the single most important thing you can learn to do to become more skilled in communication. That is why building on the love you now have is critical to improving your communication skills. When your marriage partner feels that you care, he or she will usually make efforts to communicate with you. This is another major reason why becoming a loving, caring person in marriage is so important.

What, then, is effective communication? How might it be defined? *Effective communication in a marital relationship is the ability to share information, thoughts, or feelings that are easily understood by each other.*

MEASURED HONESTY

Before we begin discussing the ways to communicate understandably, let's discuss another important issue in marital communication. The question often arises whether we should be totally open and honest with each other in marriage. Should we be able to express any thought, idea, or emotion that we feel? Should I always express exactly how I feel? Some would say yes. Others question that assumption.

If being "totally open and honest" means to not blatantly lie, cheat, or do anything that will be deceitful or cause mistrust in a marriage, then yes, it is good to be "totally open and honest." But another dimension in communication concerning honesty needs to be considered. A few years ago, many, including some of the experts, would have said, "Yes, let it all hang out. If you feel it, say it." Today, we question that philosophy. Rather than letting it "all hang out," we now advocate *measured openness and honesty* in marital communication.

Measured honesty in communication might best be explained this way. Stop for a moment and think of one of your very best friends of the same sex. Recall some of the past experiences you have had with that person. Do you appreciate having such a friend? What have you done in the past to protect or enhance the friendship?

In your conversation with that person, did you express every little petty concern that arose between you as friends? Under what circumstances was a criticism or concern discussed? Good friends usually disclose only those things to each other that are necessary to sustain and strengthen the relationship.

If a husband-wife relationship is compared to a good friendship, which it should be, we would have the same concern. What would we say, or not say, to protect the relationship? Would we air every minor concern, or would some things be best left unsaid?

Recent research has suggested that vented hostility usually generates more hostility and that repeated gripes do little to reduce the frequency or intensity of undesirable behavior. If, however, we carefully control what we say — if we measure the impact of what we share with a valued friend or spouse — the relationship will likely prosper.

With measured honesty, the question logically arises as to when to convey a concern and when to practice tolerance and restraint. If the problem continues over an extended period of time and disrupts daily routines such as sleeping, eating, and working, it should be discussed so it can be resolved. This is particularly true if the problem is becoming more and more serious. On the other hand, many of our concerns can be dealt with effectively by increasing our own level of tolerance rather than constantly demanding or expecting a marriage partner to change to meet our expectations.

Before discussing a concern, measured honesty requires that we ask these questions: Will discussing this matter improve our relationship? Will we be better off because of the disclosure? What will the impact be of what I want to say to my partner? If your relationship will benefit, then perhaps it should be discussed. If you feel your relationship will be damaged by bringing up the concern, then it's only logical not to mention it.

A successful marriage is not based on complete frankness. It is based more on sensitivity and caring, which includes a sense of when to speak up and when to practice patience and let an issue slide by.

FOUR LEVELS OF COMMUNICATION

Communication in marriage usually occurs on one of four levels: (1) things, (2) people, (3) ideas, and (4) feelings. Levels 1 and 2, things and people, usually deal with the daily routines of life. These include conversation about the weather, the ball game, children, neighbors, picking up the laundry, and topics of this nature. We can usually talk about such things in a casual and sometimes chaotic atmosphere. These are "safe" areas and require less investment of time and emotion from husbands and wives. Still, we should practice sending clear and accurate messages when conversing casually and when merely sharing information.

Levels 3 and 4, ideas and feelings, necessitate a little more preparation and planning. Expressing one's innermost thoughts when little Johnny is demanding attention or in between constant phone conversations is difficult. Often the situation must be conducive to the successful communication of ideas and feelings. The people involved in such communication must focus more carefully on what is being said.

Some men often feel more comfortable communicating on levels 1 and 2: things and people. Most women, on the other hand, like to talk on levels 3 and 4: ideas and feelings. Perhaps that is one reason why some wives often state, "We can't communicate." They may be trying to communicate ideas and feelings while their husbands are talking about things and people. With some patience, time, and skills, however, both husband and wife can learn to be more sensitive to and skilled in all of the levels.

Effective communication in marriage, especially on levels 3 and 4, has at least two important dimensions: sending clear messages and being effective listeners. Let's examine both in more detail.

SENDING CLEAR MESSAGES

When we send a message, we should first consider the two concepts of caring and measured honesty. Is your partner aware that you care about him or her? Next, measure the impact of what you are about to say. With measured honesty, you will determine if the relationship will benefit or improve because of the discussion.

When trying to send clear messages about ideas and feelings, consider the setting of your conversation, which would include both *time* and *place*. Both are equally as important as the content of the message you wish to send.

It should be obvious to most couples that certain times are more appropriate than others to discuss important matters. If a husband is irritated or annoyed and wishes to discuss the problem with his wife, he will accomplish little by trying to talk about it while she is frantically trying to get ready to go somewhere. Such conversations would be better kept for times other than when preparing income tax forms, when Aunt Tillie has come for her annual two-week visit, or when someone is suffering from fatigue, hunger, illness, sickness, exams, or other stress-creating situations. If you are tired, a few hours of sleep may help you talk more rationally and calmly.

The place you choose to have conversations on matters of major concern is important. You will need privacy, where no phone calls or knocks on the door can distract you. This can often be arranged right in your own home. But, if necessary, get away for a few hours. Go for a walk or a ride. You may want to consider going to one of your favorite restaurants for an extended conversation. Remember, try to arrange your conversations on important matters in a private, relaxed atmosphere.

In sending clear messages, think carefully about what you want to say. Just because you love each other, don't assume that the other person will automatically know your thoughts and feelings. In addition, use the word *I* rather than *you*. Learn to speak for yourself. Use phrases such as "I think . . . " or "It is my opinion . . . " In sending clear messages, don't always lay down the law of what you have to have. Appeal to the other person's sense of fairness. And if you wish to change something about your relationship, talk about what you would like in the future rather than what you don't want to continue from the past. Rather than accuse or directly confront your husband or wife on an issue, be tentative in bringing up the topic. Express your concern by beginning with the words "Is it possible that . . . " or "Could it be that . . . "

Finally, in sending clear messages, keep trying. You may have to repeat your message more than one time. The ultimate test of whether or not you have sent a clear message or messages is simply to ask your partner to repeat back what you have said. You should ask for their response before they give any comments. If the message is still unclear to them after being sent once, repeat it a second and even third time if necessary. Just remember this one principle: *The message sent is not always the message received.*

Learning to communicate understandably is well worth the effort. Successful communication requires that messages be accurately and clearly sent. And to do so takes time, thought, effort, and skill.

BEING AN EFFECTIVE LISTENER

The second important skill in effective communication is being a good listener. Of the four basic communication skills, reading, writing, speaking, and listening, research indicates that we spend 46 percent of our time listening, 30 percent of our time speaking, 15 percent of our time reading, and only 9 percent of our time writing. Yet we receive the least amount of training in the area of listening. Here, then, are nine specific techniques you can use to help you become a better listener in your marriage:

Probing. When your husband or wife is speaking, seek more information. Try to dig deeper into what your spouse is trying to say. Keep any comments you may have until later. Ask for more information by using the words *why, when, how, where,* and *what.* Try to get the other person to disclose as much as possible. Use phrases like "Tell me more," or "How did that happen?"

Clarifying. Ask your spouse to explain in more detail what he or she is trying to say. You could use phrases like "I'm not sure I understand," "Could you explain a little more about . . . ," or "Did you say . . . " Perhaps you could ask your partner to restate the position or express the concept he or she is trying to convey.

Summarizing. After your husband or wife has conveyed a particular thought or idea, summarize what you have received by saying, "What you're saying is . . . ," "What you're trying to tell me is . . . ," or "We have decided that . . . " If your summary is incomplete or inaccurate, go back to clarifying and ask your spouse to restate the point of view one more time.

Supporting. Make it clear when you agree with or at least support a spouse's statement or proposal. For instance, if a wife indicates that she needs more time alone, you might discuss it for a few minutes and then be supportive by stating, "If that's what you really need, then I think we ought to make arrangements for you to have it."

Affirming. When you feel you understand the message your spouse is making, you could indicate that by a nonverbal gesture such as nodding your head or with statements like "I agree," "That makes a lot of sense," "That's true," or "Sure."

Restating. Repeat back what has just been said. This lets your partner know what you have received and gives him or her a chance to check the clarity of the message. For example, a wife may tell her husband about a difficult moment she had that morning with their teenage daughter. The husband could say, "So you told Janet she could not go to the movie until her algebra homework was finished?" Summarizing is useful for longer messages, while restating is good for shorter messages.

Reflecting. After an exchange of information or ideas, analyze what has been said. Reflect on a few ideas that may add insight to the conversation. For example, a husband may express his desire to purchase some new fishing equipment. His wife could say, "Maybe that will help you relax and unwind a little more this summer." Perhaps she questions the proposed purchase.

Rather than just fight him on the issue, she could say, "What does that mean about the money I wanted for a new lamp and chair?"

Bouncing. This listening technique involves making a statement or quoting someone else and asking your spouse to react to the statement. For example, you might say, "Kris thinks we should go camping as a family next summer. What do you think?" Or, "Our neighbor, Bob, thinks we should have all the trees in our area sprayed for insects. How do you feel about that?"

Confronting. On occasion, you may wish to use the listening technique of confronting. Ask, in a gentle way, for a spouse to reconcile inconsistent remarks. Use phrases such as "Didn't you say before . . . " or "How do you reconcile that statement with what you said earlier?" For example, a husband may indicate the need to go out more often with his wife. When she suggests that they go to a movie that evening, he states that he is too tired. The wife may then confront him, comparing his earlier statement of the need to go out with his last statement that he is too tired to do so. Be careful with confronting that you do not provoke defensive behavior in your marriage partner.

Good listeners focus on the speakers. They turn their heads, and perhaps their chairs, in their partners' direction and look at them during the conversation. They don't stand or sit either too close or too far away. An arm's length seems to be a comfortable distance for most. They lean slightly forward in their chairs, indicating that they are listening intently. Leaning back and slouching may suggest that they are disinterested or bored.

They also listen more than they talk. Good listeners hold their own comments in reserve and encourage their partners to speak more often by using some of the techniques we have just reviewed. On occasion, they use intentional silence when they or their partners need to collect their thoughts. And finally, they use their spouses' names often without becoming overbearing or repetitious. This adds a touch of warmth since most people enjoy hearing their names used, and the use of names helps develop a sense of closeness between the people engaging in conversation. (See John W. Zehring, "Are You a Good Listener?" *Marriage and Family Living* 68, no. 3 [March 1986]: 22–25.)

NONVERBAL MESSAGES

Not all communication occurs verbally. One of the important ways we relate to others is through nonverbal messages. A touch on the shoulder may suggest concern, for instance. A slam of the door tells everyone that the person is mad. A frown shows displeasure, or concentration, or confusion, or other feelings. Sometimes the messages we send are unintentional. Following are several ways people can communicate nonverbally: voice intonation or inflection, the pace or rate of the speech, facial expressions, body posture, eye fixation or wandering, the presence or absence of touch, and, to some degree, dress and personal hygiene.

Because nonverbal messages can easily be misunderstood, couples need to exercise caution that their actions do not convey wrong messages and that they do not misread actions. If the content of a nonverbal message is critical, it can be checked out with a verbal response. For example, a husband may be explaining something of significance to his wife, but she keeps yawning. He could interpret her yawns as indications of indifference or noncaring. In reality, she could simply be tired from lack of sleep or from a particularly fatiguing day. To check the meaning of her actions, the husband may make a nonthreatening inquiry. This could begin with phrases like "I get the feeling that . . . ," "Is it possible that . . . ," "Could it be . . . ," or "You say . . . but I receive the impression that . . . "

Nonverbal cues can be an excellent way to gain insight and information into what someone else is thinking or feeling. They can also be an excellent way to reinforce messages, convey feelings, or respond to your spouse. However, always ask or "check out" your interpretation before you assume any definite meaning.

THE THREE T'S EXERCISE

One of the most effective exercises I have ever recommended to newlyweds in my classes at BYU has been the Three *T*s Exercise. The three *T*s simply stand for *time, talk,* and *touch*. I recommend that two or three times a week a couple reserve a small amount of time to talk to and touch each other. Usually it's a twenty-minute block of time in which one talks for ten minutes while the other listens and then listens while the other talks for ten minutes. This way a couple can get back in contact with each other after a hectic day. Many newly wedded couples at BYU state that they find it hard to do while in school. I suggest that if they find it difficult now, it will be even more difficult after children arrive. Truly, "as the twig is bent, the tree is inclined."

Turn off the television, put down the newspaper, put the children to bed (if you have them), and, if necessary, take the phone off the hook or turn on your answering machine. Spend the time talking about areas of mutual concern and interest. While you are talking to each other, touch each other. Hold hands or put your arms around each other in a way that demonstrates care and concern. Even twenty-minute periods with no distraction only two or three times a week help newlyweds maintain interest in their marriage. Remember, care and concern lay the foundation on which effective communication is built.

CHAPTER 9

FAMILY AND FRIENDS

When you marry, you marry the family. This simple truth is one concept I have constantly taught in my marriage classes. Not many students pay attention when I teach the idea, particularly the single students. They think they will just meet someone on campus, marry, and ride off into the sunset. As they drive off, however, they should check their rearview mirror. Because right behind them, somewhere in the dust, their family members will be following.

Many wedding ceremonies have a "giving away" part where the father of the bride or someone else "gives the bride away." That part of the ceremony is only a symbolic gesture and somewhat misleading because no parent ever totally gives a grown son or daughter away to anyone. There remains an attachment throughout life.

Some time ago I addressed a rather large LDS group on parent-child relations. During my remarks I talked about when children leave home during the late teens and how, after several vigorous years of rearing children, my wife and I were looking forward to that in many ways. After I finished, an elderly man came up and in half jest said, "For someone with a Ph.D., you have something yet to learn about families. Children never leave home. They may move several miles away, even to another country, but they are always with you in thought no matter where they go." He said that there is another dimension of parent-child relationships after the teen years are over.

TWO COMMANDMENTS:
HONORING PARENTS AND LEAVING PARENTS

I remember when I received my patriarchal blessing at the age of sixteen. In my blessing, the patriarch, Charles S. Hansen, admonished that I should always seek the advice of my parents. When my blessing was finished, he commented, "Brent, you noted that the Lord told you to always seek the advice of your parents." I said that I understood. I intended to do that for the next few years until I was old enough to leave home.

"That is not what your blessing meant," he cautioned. "The Lord meant for you to seek the advice of your parents even after you leave home." For several months after that, I pondered over my blessing. Why should adult children seek the advice of parents once they have left home? At that point I began to better understand one of the Ten Commandments: "Honour thy father and thy mother." (Ex. 20:12.)

Adult sons and daughters can learn a great deal from parents even after leaving home. I learned this shortly after we were married. A man came to our home one evening with a "once in a lifetime" investment opportunity in some questionable stocks. The only catch was that we had to invest several thousand dollars (which we didn't have) within forty-eight hours in order to take advantage of the "opportunity." It sounded too good to be true, which we have since learned is a tip-off against investments. He wanted us to borrow the money and sign the contract the next day. We were tempted.

He said he'd call back the following afternoon for our answer and, he hoped, our money. I couldn't sleep that night. Should we borrow the money and invest? What if we missed a true opportunity, as the man had suggested we might? But how much risk was involved in the investment? What should we do?

The next morning, following the counsel in my patriarchal blessing many years earlier, I called Dad on the phone. He listened for a few minutes and said that he couldn't tell me what to do (which is a good strategy for in-laws and family) but that he would be careful if he were in my place. First, he said, I should be cautious about borrowing money to invest unless I could afford to lose it all. We couldn't afford it. Then, he said, anytime anyone puts a time clause on a sale, such as "you must act within so many hours," you had better be cautious. "If the offer isn't good a week from now, it isn't all that good now."

The advice of my father that day helped me decide not to invest and subsequently not to lose several thousand dollars, which is what happened to the man and many other investors who decided to "act now." Because parents have had many more experiences in life, they can often teach young adults what they have learned, protecting their children even after they are grown. Perhaps that is what the blessing for honoring one's parents refers to: "That thy days may be long upon the land." (Ex. 20:12.)

Obviously, young married couples are under no obligation to follow their parents' counsel or even to listen. But occasionally seeking the advice of parents, especially as untried newly married couples just starting out, is one way we can both honor them and benefit.

The scriptures also teach that we should "leave" father and mother. (Gen. 2:24.) Is it possible to do both: honor one's parents and leave them? I think so. And doing both may well be the key to stable family and in-law relationships once we have married and left home. I have known many young people who have left home and yet do not honor their parents. Some haven't talked to their parents or seen them for years. Still others continue to honor father and mother after marriage but in a real sense do not leave them.

I know a marriage-and-family counselor who lived in Utah for several years and who was not a Latter-day Saint. During his time in Utah, he counseled many LDS families. When he decided to leave our area, I asked him what observations he had about working with Latter-day Saints. He was very complimentary but said that he had observed one peculiarity. Many LDS families are so close-knit in the name of family solidarity that they have a difficult time letting go of their children once they grow up and leave home. Some LDS children are unable to cope well with life once they leave home because they never, in a sense, leave father and mother. He suggested that this was not in the best interest of either the child or the parent. He said that he had often performed a "parentectomy," or a removal of the parent from the child, right in his office during therapy.

Once children leave father and mother, they are free to return for the needed continued relationship. I have often suggested to many young people that they leave home as a child and then return as a friend. I don't know of a better relationship for a couple to have with their parents once they are married than being good friends.

One of the keys for a stable relationship with parents and in-laws during the early years of marriage is to observe the simple principle of the Golden Mean: *Not too much and not too little.* For a couple after marriage trying to establish a proper relationship with parents, it means not too much and not too little involvement. We have so much invested in family relationships prior to marriage that we continue to need and to want the relationships to continue after marriage. The key is to strike a balance in how much involvement to have. If we have too little involvement with parents and siblings, we alienate them and contribute to unneeded friction and to hurt feelings. If we have too much involvement, we can experience dissension in our own marital relationship.

Late one night a young man called on the phone and got me out of bed. He said that he had been married just a few months but was upset because his wife was going home to visit her mother and father for two weeks. I asked him why that bothered him, and he said that daughters shouldn't have to return home once they are married. Upon further questioning, I found that the young bride hadn't been to see her parents since the wedding.

"And besides," the young groom said, "how can she stand to be away from me for two weeks?" The more he talked, the more I understood how she could stand it. She needed to get away! I finally convinced the anxious young husband that time spent away from each other need not be disruptive to a marriage. Much of it depends on the motive for leaving and the amount of time spent away from each other. In fact, time wisely invested in relationships with family members and friends can be a boost to the marriage.

An important step to striking the balance is to talk about the situation with one's spouse. How does he or she feel about family/in-law interaction? Is it too much? Too little? Is there a need for more or less involvement? If a young husband and wife keep each other first in priority in all aspects of life, including relationships with family and friends, yet establish proper priorities for extended family ties, the marriage has a good chance of prospering.

Contrary to popular opinion, many young married couples have very good relationships with their family members and in-laws. In fact, some spouses get along better with in-laws than with their own parents. My estimates over the years have been that about half of the married couples get along reasonably well with in-laws. But the other half have problems ranging anywhere from minimal to severe. By themselves, some young couples often get along well, only to find that one of their parents is a "smother" or a "bother" rather than a mother or a father. Leaving home then becomes more of a process than an event. But this adjustment, like most others we encounter in marriage, usually works out in time if both husband and wife conscientiously try to resolve it. In fact, many young couples perceive parents and in-laws to be a stabilizing influence and a blessing in their lives rather than the stereotypes promoted in the media and in print.

Unlike the image perpetuated in jokes, comic strips, and other media, in-law adjustments are usually between the new bride and her mother-in-law rather than between the groom and his mother-in-law. A mother generally tends to be a little closer to her children than the father is and sometimes has a more difficult time letting go. Young brides should be wary about taking this problem personally since any other young woman who married the son would likely be undergoing similar adjustment. Just remember. Every girl marries some mother's son. And someday, in turn, that girl will probably see a young girl marry one of her sons as well. At that later time, she may have a better understanding of the difficulty of a mother letting go of a son or daughter.

There are also some stressful moments during the engagement and first few months of marriage in trying to figure out how to address one's in-laws. Do you call them "Mom and Dad"? Some do. Others can't because they believe that Mom and Dad designate specific people. They may experiment with "Mr. and Mrs.," "Brother and Sister," first names, or nicknames. Others are so confused that they don't know how to address in-laws, so they just wait until they are looking in their direction and start talking (the "Hey, you" phenomenon). This problem is alleviated somewhat after the first child is born and they are simply called Grandpa or Grandma.

As we get older, our parents will need us in special ways. First, they just want to be part of our lives and know that they did an adequate job in rearing us. This is a rather simple task for married children to accomplish. Just reassure both sets of parents that you appreciate what they have done for you thus far in life. To in-laws, you can express appreciation to them for having provided you with a fine husband or wife. Some young couples, either before or shortly after the marriage, write a letter of appreciation to in-laws stating such sentiments. Later in life, a few parents may need financial assistance in meeting the heavy medical bills and other obligations that come with aging. Finally, as mortality draws to a close, they will need you, as you will also need others when you become feeble and approach death.

FRIENDSHIPS AFTER MARRIAGE

Mutual friends can be a great source of support after we are married. But do we both enjoy the same people as friends? How much time should we spend with them? How much say-so do spouses have with their partner's involvement with friends? When do we invite them over to our home? Who decides? How much involvement, if any, should we have with former boyfriends or girlfriends? Should we even allow ourselves to think about them?

About one year after Susan and I were married, Susan said halfway through dinner that she had something to tell me. I asked her what it was. She replied that, on occasion, she still thought about former boyfriends.

You may think that I became furious. I did not. In fact, it was somewhat of a relief. Because I had something I had been wanting to tell my new wife but somehow didn't know how to—I had sometimes thought about former girlfriends too.

We had a good laugh about it that evening because both of us had experienced it but didn't know how to tell the other. And in hindsight, I don't know if we should have even tried to discuss it prior to that point. I don't know if either of us would have been mature enough to handle it during the first few precarious months of marriage.

I'm not recommending that young husbands and wives sit down and discuss how they felt or still may feel about former relationships. One of the vows in many marriage ceremonies is that we "forsake all others." This forsaking is social, physical, and mental. Our marriage vows imply that we will focus our time, attention, and energies on each other and not on former relationships or on relationships that may develop after we are married.

So much for the ideal. The reality is that, like Susan and myself, most married couples come into marriage having had a variety of dating relationships. I don't know how accurate the figure is, but I have often guessed that as many as 80 percent of the people who marry do not marry the first person they fall in love with. If that statistic is even close, it means that the great majority of couples face the sensitive issue of discussing or even mentioning former boyfriends or girlfriends.

A few years ago Susan gave me one of the nicest gifts I have ever received for Christmas. She had gotten out all the pictures my father and mother had given us of my years at home. Then Susan organized them into two scrapbooks by category and year. It was sort of a "This Is Your Life, Brent Barlow."

I was overwhelmed with the gift and very pleased. As I looked through it that Christmas morning, I came to one section titled "Girl Friends." I glanced through the pages that followed and found a wide array of pictures of young women I had dated in high school and college. I asked Susan if that section was difficult to put together. She said something that morning that impressed me. She said, "No, as I was putting your scrapbook together, I realized that your dating years were an important part of your life. I didn't want to leave them out."

I squirmed a bit. I didn't know if I could have been mature enough to have done the same thing for her. Then she said, "Besides, these young women helped you grow up and learn about life . . . and love. They helped prepare you for me." What a nice thing for a wife to say to her husband! Remember, this was some twenty years after we were married. I wonder if I could give Susan a gift like that even now. I am somewhat more jealous. Susan had a lot of boyfriends during high school and college. (I suspect, in fact, that at one time she had a 1-800 telephone number for dating.)

A few years ago, while speaking to an LDS group in another state, I saw in the audience a woman I had dated during my college days. In fact, we had become quite serious, but obviously the relationship had not led to marriage. Now, some fifteen years later, we met again, both having married other people, and this was the first time we had seen each other since that time.

I lost my concentration in my speech but somehow got through it. When it was over, she came up to the podium and introduced herself and her husband whom I had never met. We went through the small talk, and then she said something that I appreciated very much, "I think I am a better person for having dated you in college." What a wonderful compliment! I realized too that I was a better person because of the relationship. That incident, I think, reflects something that is true for most of us. Former serious relationships that do not lead to marriage are usually not lost causes. We learn. We grow. We mature. And life continues. Perhaps we all should be thankful to the young men or women who previously dated our spouses and helped them learn about love and life.

Susan and I apparently are not the only couple who have had to deal with former boyfriends and girlfriends. When I was writing my weekly column for the *Deseret News* I received a letter in the mail from a young LDS wife. She wrote:

> Dear Dr. Barlow,
>
> My husband and I have been married for about two years, and everything has been going fine expect for one thing. I keep thinking about a fellow to whom I was engaged before I met my husband. I find myself thinking about him from time to time and even dream about him on occasion. Is this normal, or is there something wrong with me? Does it mean anything about my present relationship with my husband? Could it be disruptive to my marriage?

Here is my answer:

You are quite normal, and your situation is fairly common since the vast majority of us usually become involved in one or two romantic relationships that do not lead to marriage. The impact of a former relationship on marriage, other than divorce, is one of the most neglected areas in marriage and family studies.

I have seen some young people become so devastated from breaking off an engagement that they take months to recover. Some never recover at all and choose to remain single the rest of their lives rather than risk the pain of separation again. After breaking up, some will quickly get into another relationship to show themselves, friends and family, or their former boy- or girlfriend that they are capable of loving and being loved again. Some of these off-the-rebound relationships lead to marriage and often end up with disastrous consequences. While divorce therapy has become more prominent during the past few years, we have not given enough attention to helping people get out of relationships before marriage.

A few husbands and wives find themselves attracted to other men and women after marriage. Whatever the reasons, they feel that if they remain attracted to other people than their spouses, they are not now in love and should terminate their marriages. Some have naïvely done so, only to find after another marriage that they continue to be attracted to others. Rather than chase butterflies and seek happiness elsewhere, many of us should examine our situation, learn to be content, and seek happiness in our present marriage.

Some married women, and I suppose married men, retain mementos from former boyfriends and girlfriends. And if they do not retain the mementos, they retain the memories. Some keep old love letters, pictures, rings, or gifts for sentimental reasons. When the present relationship becomes shaky, out come the items as a means of solace and a reminder that someone once loved them, and perhaps still does.

While retaining pleasant thoughts of a former relationship may be somewhat normal, we should be careful not to let them interfere with our marriage. The thoughts are usually harmless unless one chooses to dwell on them often or for extended periods. This phenomenon, known as psychic infidelity or mental wanderlust, can be highly disruptive to a marriage, especially if one wonders how a marriage to the person may have been if things had worked out otherwise.

You need not try to totally forget your former boyfriend, nor need you feel guilty or ashamed because of him. The time you spent together was not wasted even though you did not marry. You both matured and contributed to each other's lives at that particular time.

But since you did not marry each other, you should reexamine your present commitment to your husband and remember your wedding vows. The total efforts of both husband and wife are needed in contemporary marriage to meet the daily demands of life. All the time and energy invested in others only serve to undermine your present marital relationship.

If necessary, burn some of your old love letters from him if you still have them. Perhaps gifts and other mementos should also be discarded if they are interfering with your marriage.

Be careful not to fan the spark of an old flame. While fire may provide warmth and comfort, it can also be consuming.

Thanks for your letter.

Sincerely,

Brent A. Barlow

CHAPTER 10

WHEN CHANGE IS NECESSARY

The bliss and romance newlyweds enjoy usually continue well into the first year of marriage. In my marriage classes at BYU, I can look out over the students and tell who has been married for the shortest period of time. They will be sitting close to each other, hugging each other, kissing each other "hello" or "good bye" as the class begins or ends. And their comments in class usually indicate that they have a very rosy picture of what lies ahead of them in marriage.

The couples who are past their first year of marriage, however, know that things are not quite the same as they were at the time of the wedding or the period shortly after. In fact, there are some indications that the first six months of marriage is the idyllic period. During the last six months of the first year, newlyweds begin to realize that things are not quite as they used to be or were expected to be. Also about this time, young couples begin to think that some changes need to be made.

Change is a somewhat threatening aspect of marriage for many husbands and wives. This is particularly so for many LDS couples. I have often wondered why. For one thing, we choose someone for marriage because of certain traits or characteristics they possess. And we don't want them to change because of the very things that attracted us to them. Some husbands, for instance, do not want wives to change their hairstyle or manner of dress. They want them to look and dress the way they did when they were first married. Consequently, some wives keep hairstyles and clothing that are outdated. Some wives, on the other hand, do not want husbands to develop new hobbies, relationships with male friends, or other interests outside the home because such things may take them away from the home and marriage.

There are numerous other reasons why husbands and wives are hesitant to experience change in their marriages. And some concern is warranted. We would not want a spouse to change in a way that may be inconsistent with gospel principles or may, in fact, be against the law. These changes, however, are the exception rather than the rule. The changes I am talking about are changes in such things as clothing preferences, hairstyle, occupational or educational pursuits, or other areas affected by aging.

RESISTANCE TO CHANGE

I have also come to realize that there are some interesting religious factors for Latter-day Saints that may inhibit change. One is the concept about deity, stated in the scriptures, that the Lord is "the same yesterday, to-day, and forever." (1 Ne. 10:18; see also 2 Ne. 27:23; 29:9; Alma 31:17.) In efforts to become more Christlike or Godlike, some LDS couples interpret this to mean that since the Lord is unchanging, they should be likewise. The only problem is that God is at a state of perfection, where change is unnecessary. As imperfect mortals, however, married couples should be willing to make appropriate changes and adjustments to preserve and strengthen marriage and family relationships. Eternal progression and repentance also necessitate some changes.

Another aspect of change is reflected in one of our Church hymns. In a church service not long ago, as the congregation was singing "Abide with Me," a particular phrase caught my attention: "Earth's joys grow dim; its glories pass away. Change and decay in all around I see; O thou who changest not, abide with me." (*Hymns,* 1985, no. 166.) Henry F. Lyte, who wrote the words to "Abide with Me," equated change with decay in this hymn. His thinking may have reflected his times and suggests that things were better during a former period. Situations and people supposedly become worse after changes occur.

The tendency to idealize the past—the way things have been—was not peculiar to Henry F. Lyte. Nor was it restricted to religious thought. There is a tendency to do the same with marriage and family life. It is what they call "the western family of nostalgia."

We tend to look to the past and long for previous times. Family life was supposedly best many years ago, during pioneer times and up through the postdepression era. Popular television programs in the past like "The Waltons" and "Little House on the Prairie" have emphasized these beliefs by portraying close, loving families from earlier periods. Some people still believe that marriage and family life were best then, and any change from that era has supposedly only brought about disorganization and chaos, even decay. Once again, any change or departure from the past is only thought to be for the worse.

If we had to choose, would many of us actually return to the past and live then? Must marriage and family life be exactly as it was in the past? Can change be for the better? I believe it can. The environment and society do not necessarily determine family life. The principles, not the times, create close, loving relationships. Conscientious choice and effort make change positive no matter the time and place.

Perhaps another reason we are afraid of change is because we do not want to risk anything. We do not want to upset the status quo, even if the status quo is less than desirable. In trying to change, we may lose something we have. In being willing to risk, however, we may gain something we don't have.

97

The necessity of risk and change in life is noted in these few lines by an unknown author:

To laugh is to risk appearing the fool,
To weep is to risk appearing sentimental,
To reach out for another is to risk involvement,
To expose feeling is to risk exposing your true self,
To place your ideas, your dreams before the crowd is to risk their loss,
To love is to risk not being loved in return,
To live is to risk dying,
To hope is to risk despair,
To try is to risk failure;
But risk must be taken, because the greatest hazard in life is to risk nothing.
The person who risks nothing does nothing, has nothing, and is nothing.
He may avoid suffering and sorrow, but he simply cannot learn, feel,
    change, grow, love, live.
Chained by his certitudes, he is a slave, he has forfeited freedom.
Only a person who risks—is free.

And may I add, only the person who risks can grow . . . and change.

CAN'T, WON'T, AND DON'T

There are three words that I hear often from husbands and wives who are describing their marital relationship: *can't*, *won't*, and *don't*. Wives will often say something like "My husband can't communicate," or "He won't help around the house." Husbands may say things like "She just won't be affectionate," or "Wives can't understand certain things about men." The three words surface in countless other sentences of husbands and wives. This may seem trivial to others, but I think that the ways these three words are used are very important.

For instance, suppose a wife feels that her husband is inattentive to her emotional needs. She tries to express herself to him, but there is no reciprocation. She could say any of the following to her husband:

"You can't help me with my emotional needs."

"You won't help me with my emotional needs."

"You do not help me with my emotional needs."

The statement "You can't . . . " suggests that the husband neither has nor will ever develop the skills necessary to relate to her emotional needs. It is as if he does not have the capability to do it. Using "You can't . . . " statements is a judgment or an assessment of what an individual can and can not do.

The statement "You won't . . . " is an evaluation of stubbornness, indicating an unwillingness to do something that one is capable of doing. It is an accusation that the other has made a conscious decision not to do something.

The statement "You don't . . . " again is an evaluation, but one that can be based on more empirical evaluation. A phrase such as "You don't help enough with the housework" can more easily be verified and documented than the accusation "You won't help with housework."

As husbands and wives, we need to be careful how we use these three words. Remember: *can't* suggests the lack of skills, *won't* suggests unwillingness or stubbornness, and *don't* observes a lack of activity that can be verified. In relating concerns about your marriage, be careful in distinguishing between (1) inability, (2) unwillingness, and (3) infrequency.

If you seldom or infrequently go out as a couple, let that be the issue rather than cloud the point by bringing up inability or unwillingness. If you would like to share more frequent or more caring intimate moments in your marriage, discuss that rather than bring in the issue of the other person's supposed inability or stubbornness to do so.

I believe that most husbands and wives have the skills and capability to live in stable and satisfying marital relationships. One problem is that they often do not apply or use the skills and resources they already have. *Can't, won't,* and *don't* — three important words in contemporary marriage. Be careful how you use them in yours.

CHANGING ONESELF IS DIFFICULT FOR MANY

I'm absolutely amazed at how resistant many are to change even when they know it would be in their best interests. They will say things like "You can't teach old dogs new tricks," or "You can't change the spots on a leopard's back." And in some ways these statements are true because they refer to someone trying to change someone else. It is becoming more and more evident that one person cannot change another. Manipulation, force, or coercion can bring about momentary change. There is a saying that reflects the depth of such change: "A person convinced against his will is of the same opinion still." Yet many continue to try changing their partners rather than themselves.

Even though it is difficult, if not impossible, for one person to change another, the vital truth is that people can change themselves. In fact, when they choose to do so, many individuals have made remarkable changes in their lives.

In counseling sessions, people often argue, sometimes rather heatedly, about why they can't change. They will cite reasons such as their childhood, family background, or previous painful relationships in life. They give arguments about their birth order, convinced that because they are a second or third child, they are authorized to act in a certain way even if it is detrimental to the relationship. Some note that they were born under a certain sign, like Taurus or Gemini, and believe that such signs govern their actions. They check their horoscope each day in the newspaper to see how they are going to behave. Others have even visited palm readers or will relate a certain mystic or religious experience that implies that they are to be or act a certain way.

A few will ascribe their inability to change to certain physical or medical impairments. In a number of these cases, there is some validity to the claims. Even so, I believe that such individuals must accept some responsibility, not so much for the physical impairment, but for their response or reaction to it.

Before we decide we "can't" or "won't" change something in our marriage, we should remember the story about a scorpion and a frog.

They met on a river bank one day, and both needed to cross the river. The scorpion said, "Let me get on your back, and you can give me a ride to the other side."

"But if I did," said the frog, "you would sting me, and I would die."

"But if I sting you," replied the scorpion, "I will drown with you."

After some thought the frog said, "You're right. Get on my back, and I'll take you across the river."

The scorpion got on the frog's back, but halfway across the river, the scorpion stung the frog on the neck. The frog became paralyzed, and they both began to sink. The frog gasped, "Why did you do that?"

Just before they both drowned in the river, the scorpion replied, "I had to. It's just my nature."

In order to change a marriage, married couples must first believe that change is possible. Otherwise, they just continue in the punitive, unsatisfying behavior that may even be paralyzing the relationship. And eventually they too emotionally sink and drown.

Sometimes the resistance to change is so pronounced that troubled young couples continue to punish and hurt each other even though they know that change is vital and in their best interest. They think they have to continue to inflict pain and hurt each other. These couples foolishly believe that they just can't change. It's not their nature.

101

FIVE SCRIPTURES THAT CAN CHANGE YOUR MARRIAGE

Think for a moment of ways your marriage might be changed for the good. I will now outline five scriptures that are guaranteed to help you change if you apply them as suggested. They are guaranteed because the Lord has given them and promises that they will work. I have lectured often on these five scriptures and have heard some interesting reports of their impact on contemporary living.

Scripture #1: Matthew 7:12. The Law of the Boomerang.

Most people know Matthew 7:12 as the Golden Rule: "Whatsoever ye would that men should do to you, do ye even so to them." (See also Luke 6:31.) Do to others as you would have them do to you; treat others as you would like to be treated. Such conduct will allow a person to get along in life with most people.

There is another principle, however, contained in Matthew 7:12 that I call the law of the boomerang. The lesson is this: Think how you would like to be treated, treat another that way first, and eventually the behavior will be returned to you by others, as will a well-thrown boomerang. When I was a freshman enrolled at BYU, I remember a returned missionary from Australia who took us out to the field north of Helaman Halls late one afternoon and demonstrated how to throw boomerangs. He had large ones and small ones. But each boomerang thrown, regardless of size, would go out in some sort of irregular pattern and then return to our position nearly every time.

The principle in human relationships is that you, and not the other person in the relationship, have to start the process of desirable change. You have to be willing to exert some effort in order to bring about the kind of relationship you desire. Other scriptures contain similar thoughts. Jesus declared, "With what measure ye mete, it shall be measured to you again." (Matt. 7:2.) In the book of Luke, we read, "Give, and it shall be given unto you." (6:38.) The writer of Ecclesiastes wrote, "Cast thy bread upon the waters: for thou shalt find it after many days." (11:1.) Alma likewise declared to his son Corianton, "For that which ye do send out shall return unto you again." (Alma 41:15.)

Scripture #2: Matthew 7:3–5. The Change-First Principle.

For some reason, a great many people will wait for someone else to change first. "I will change after he/she changes" is a comment often heard in marriage counseling where couples come to confess each other's sins. In the Sermon on the Mount, Jesus asked, "Why beholdest thou the mote that is in thy brother's [or spouse's] eye, but considerest not the beam that is in thine own eye? Or how wilt thou say to thy brother [or husband or wife], Let me pull out the mote out of thine eye; and, behold, a beam is in thine own eye?" (Matt. 7:3–4.) By trade, Jesus was a carpenter and used a carpenter's analogy of a mote (a speck) and a beam to describe the degree of inaccuracy with which we see inadequacies in ourselves and in others. He then charged: "Thou hypocrite, first cast out the beam out of thine own eye; and then shalt thou see clearly to cast out the mote out of thy brother's eye." (Matt. 7:5.)

Jesus simply acknowledged the common human tendency of waiting for the other person to initiate the change. He admonished that, rather than wait, we not only initiate the change, but also start by working on our own imperfections. Then our perception of other people's weaknesses will be dramatically altered.

Not long ago I was speaking to a rather large group about marriage. On the front row was an elderly couple who were having a hard time hearing, so I tried to speak a little louder than normal. During the speech I talked about the change-first principle as an important part of marital relationships. At the end of my speech, the older couple came up to the rostrum. The man shook my hand and said, "Dr. Barlow, you have just solved a major problem we have had for years in our marriage." He then turned to his wife and said rather sternly, "Did you hear Dr. Barlow, dear? If we want a better marriage, you have to be willing to change first!"

As long as husbands and wives focus on and emphasize each other's faults and imperfections, they will make no real progress in changing their relationships. The almost universal reaction is that when a relationship is impaired, each spouse thinks the other is at fault. We can nag, complain, hint, bribe, insult, or even try to physically force the other to change. But as we soon learn, it is to no avail.

The only real, genuine, lasting change that occurs in a marriage, or any other relationship for that matter, is that which is self-instigated. Change from within. You can, as a marriage partner, invite (not demand) the other to change. But even in that case, you must be willing to change first. If you want a better relationship with your spouse, or with anyone else for that matter, you have to initiate the desired changes by working on yourself first. If you are going to reform your marriage, let the reformation begin with you! Get a mirror rather than a magnifying glass.

Scripture #3: Galatians 6:7. The Law of the Harvest.

Another simple but somewhat controversial biblical passage says, "Whatsoever a man soweth, that shall he also reap." (Gal. 6:7.) It means that whatever you do in life will yield something.

The controversial part of the scripture is that things often happen to individuals that have nothing to do with previous effort or the lack of it. Sometimes bad things happen to good people, problems for which they are not responsible. The scripture, however, does not say that everything a man experiences is a result of something he does, but rather what a man does has consequences that return.

Some women at my BYU Education Week lectures have become upset when we read the law of the harvest and apply it to marriage. They will later argue that they are in difficult marriages right now for which they do not feel responsible. And I can understand their feelings. I have suggested to those experiencing difficulties that, even if they have not sown the seeds of disharmony or discontent in their marriages, they at least have nurtured the process once it is underway. When they react, their reaction will inevitably yield something they reap. The bad news of the law of the harvest is that the results of our actions can be negative: "For they have sown the wind, and they shall reap the whirlwind." (Hosea 8:7.)

The good news is that if we want to reap more harmony and satisfaction out of the relationship, we have to sow the seeds that will bring that harvest about. And the promise is that eventually we will reap, in a positive way, what we take the time to sow. Many married couples today, as well as parents, are hesitant to do good to another person (plant the seeds) when difficulties arise. We are not sure "good will be returned for good," nor do we believe that anything positive will result if we display love and kindness when it seemingly is not warranted by another. Latter-day revelation urges, "Fear not to do good, . . . for whatsoever ye sow, that shall ye also reap; therefore, if ye sow good ye shall also reap good for your reward. Therefore, fear not, little flock; do good." (D&C 6:33–34.)

Scripture #4: James 1:4. The Patience Principle.

James urges that we "let patience have her perfect work." (James 1:4.) Not everything worthwhile we do in life will have immediate rewards or a prompt impact. During the long hot days of summer, for example, I will often walk through our garden and say to myself, "No growth . . . no growth." Later that evening, we will have a family home evening. The kids may not listen attentively to the lesson or may even appear uninterested. As we conclude, I may likewise say to myself, "No growth . . . no growth." Yet Susan and I know the growth process is under way both in our garden and with our children, even though the growth may seem slow and is not readily discernible. We have had to learn the patience principle in both gardening and parenting.

In the intermountain area, we are accustomed to short growing seasons of just a few months. We plant in the spring and reap in the fall of the same year. But both the law of the harvest and the patience principle suggest that we may have to plant and then water and weed for an extended period of time before the harvest will occur. It is true in gardening and is also true in some aspects of marriage and family relationships.

When Susan and I were in Hawaii recently, we wanted to visit a macadamia nut farm. We drove to one and saw a big sign that read, "We are sorry, but we are out of macadamia nuts. It takes seven years from the time you plant until you reap a harvest. We are now in our sixth year. Come back next year, and we will have macadamia nuts."

While we were in Hawaii, we also learned that it takes eighteen months to reap the first crop of pineapples and thirty months to reap the second. The planting, nurturing, and harvest season for pineapples lasts nearly three years. I also understand it takes twenty years before the first crop of olives can be picked, and forty years before the olive trees fully mature.

If we want to reap a reward in this life or the next, we must understand the growth process and learn to be patient with ourselves and our loved ones. Between the planting and the harvest, we will continue to nurture, water, and weed whether growing olives . . . or rearing children . . . or being married. We will continue to have faith in the growth process, however long it takes.

Scripture #5: Doctrine and Covenants 1:10. The Divine Promise.

Some people with whom I have shared these five principles and scriptures wonder if the processes implied really work. I assure them that they will and that they always have . . . when properly applied. But if we are afraid to initiate the effort, change first, plant the seeds of harmony, and nurture them with patience, we should examine the Lord's promises of rewards, justice, and mercy. He declared, speaking of the last days, "Unto the day when the Lord shall come to recompense unto every man according to his work, and measure to every man according to the measure which he has measured to his fellow man." (D&C 1:10.)

If we are kind, patient, considerate, and loving toward others, and they do not respond favorably at all, even during this lifetime, our efforts are not wasted or in vain. The Lord has said that he will treat us and ultimately judge us by the same standard we have accorded others. The boomerang will return, and we will ultimately reap a harvest. It is a divine promise.

THE PRINCIPLES IN ACTION

One time when I was in Denver, Colorado, I shared these five scriptures and concepts with an LDS audience. At the conclusion of the meeting, a father in his midforties came up to the podium.

He tearfully shared with me a rather unpleasant experience he had had with his teenage son that very day. It was just one of many difficult experiences during the previous three years. The son had left home more than once and had done many things inconsistent with LDS values. The father was so exasperated that Saturday morning that he had decided to hear my lecture that evening. Then he would go home and, I quote, "lay down the law" to his son. He had even written several items on a 3" x 5" card that he would insist his son do in order to remain at home. "The main thing I want from my son, Dr. Barlow," he said, "is for him to respect and value my opinions."

He continued. "As you reviewed those five principles tonight, the law of the boomerang, the change-first principle, the law of the harvest, the patience principle, and the divine promise, I paid attention. For the first time

107

I realized that I could expect nothing from my son that I was not willing to do . . . first. If I want him to respect and value my opinions, then I will have to first respect and value his opinions."

During my speech that night, he had written ideas on the other side of the 3" x 5" card. He said that he was going to go home and tell his son what he, the father, was willing to do to change the relationship. He would explain that he was willing to change first. In addition, he wanted to test the law of the harvest, be patient, and hope for the divine promise.

I don't know what happened that night when the father returned home. I do know, however, that the son was not forced out prematurely. And the father was willing to work on himself first for improvements in his relationship with his wayward son.

One of the most dramatic applications of these five scriptures I've heard about was by an older LDS sister and her husband. I had given a lecture in her stake during an Education Weekend in which I shared the five scriptures and principles.

At the end of the series, she came up and gave me a hug. She said she appreciated my comments but was not sure about the change-first principle. They had been married more than fifty years, and she said she couldn't remember the last time her husband had told her he loved her. (Why some LDS men do not, or cannot, or will not say, "I love you," to their wives is one of the great mysteries of life.)

She told me that she had tried everything possible she knew of to get him to tell her he loved her. But she had gotten no results. And she said, "Dr. Barlow, I had decided that I would not tell him I love him until he told me first!"

She then commented on what we had discussed that evening. According to the principles, if she wanted her husband to tell her he loved her, she would have to be willing to tell him . . . first. She said she didn't think it would work but would go home and try. Then she would write and let me know what happened.

About a year later I received a letter from the woman. She wrote that she had gone home that night and told her husband that she loved him. His only response was "Thanks." The next morning at breakfast, she also conveyed the same sentiment, and he simply said, "OK." She indicated in her letter that she got out paper and a pen right then to write and tell me that the law of the boomerang and change-first principle didn't work. Then she remembered the patience principle and decided to try it several more times during the next few weeks before she gave up.

A few days later her husband had a heart attack. He had not been in good health for several months. Every day she went to the intensive care unit at the local hospital to visit him. He was awake and could talk but was in critical condition. Every time she went to the hospital to see her ailing husband, she told him she loved him. He thanked her each time but said nothing in return.

One night she was sitting in his room in the hospital. He was becoming weaker by the hour. That night he motioned for her to come over to his side. He took her hand and called her by name, then said, "I want you to know . . . at this time . . . that I love you." She said that they both knew what "at this time" meant. He acknowledged that he had heard her declarations of love during those previous few weeks. But for some reason, he had a hard time telling her that he also loved her. Nevertheless, he knew that he needed to tell her so that evening.

In the final paragraph of her letter, the woman noted that her husband died just a few hours later. But she was grateful that, before he died, she had heard from his own lips that he loved her. And she thanked me once again for sharing with her a few scriptural principles that helped bring it about.

Newlyweds need not wait till they are older to start applying the five principles. They can learn to exchange words of endearment and give gifts such as flowers to their husbands or wives while they are still alive. They can incorporate changes in themselves to bring about greater caring, harmony, peace, and joy. If they sow good seeds early, there will be time not only to experience early fruit, but also to savor the later fruit.

CHAPTER 11

THE HIGHS AND LOWS OF MARRIED LIFE

During the years that I have been teaching Family Science 301, "Preparation for Marriage," at BYU, some genuinely humorous things have happened. One incident in particular comes to mind.

Each semester I tell my students that there is an important biblical verse regarding preparation for marriage called the parable of the tower, found in Luke 14:28–30. It teaches that we should evaluate the amount of energy, time, and "costs" of major projects before we undertake them.

One day in class I asked for a volunteer to read this particular scripture and try to relate it to contemporary marriage. One young coed volunteered, but instead of turning to Luke 14, the young woman mistakenly turned to Luke 13. She then began reading verse 28, which states, "There shall be weeping and gnashing of teeth"! We had a good laugh about the biblical "insight" on contemporary marriage.

On another occasion my phone rang late at night. This time one of my former students was on the other end of the line. "Can we talk for a few minutes, Dr. Barlow?" she asked.

I glanced at my watch and said yes.

"Marriage is nothing like I thought it would be," she started. She cried as she documented her disappointment with her husband and their relationship. She said that he was not like he was when they were first married. He now

111

left his clothes lying around and was less attentive. And they were rapidly running out of money. Finally I stopped her long enough to ask, "Just how long have you been married anyway?"

"Two weeks!" she sobbed.

I told her not to give up because her marriage would likely get better day by day. What my young student was experiencing is fairly common to most married couples. There are usually some highs and some lows in married life. Her first low came rather early.

Almost all of us can recall some difficult moments we have had during our years of marriage. And perhaps we, as did my student, despair on occasion during those times. But the difficult times do not necessarily indicate that we love each other less. They could just as easily indicate that we've had better times before and likely will experience better times again.

Dwelling too much on the lows is dangerous and harmful. The more we worry about what is wrong with our relationship, the lower we seem to sink; and the more we remind ourselves how bad things are or have been, the more likely we are to begin to gauge our entire marriage by the lows—even the lows of the lows.

One of the peculiar dynamics of a couple's relationship when they are contemplating divorce is that they're usually preoccupied with what is wrong with their marriage. Each person can document the times and places that the marriage began to suffer. But they seldom stop to remember and relive together the highs—the good times, the happy moments, the experiences that increased their love for each other.

Relatively few of us can continuously maintain a happily-ever-after type of marriage. President Spencer W. Kimball once noted:

> Two people coming from different backgrounds soon learn after the ceremony is performed that stark reality must be faced. There is no longer

a life of fantasy or of make-believe; we must come out of the clouds and put our feet firmly on the earth. Responsibility must be assumed and new duties must be accepted. Some personal freedoms must be relinquished and many adjustments, unselfish adjustments, must be made.

One comes to realize very soon after marriage that the spouse has weaknesses not previously revealed or discovered. The virtues that were constantly magnified during courtship now grow relatively smaller, and the weaknesses that seemed so small and insignificant during courtship now grow to sizeable proportions. The hour has come for understanding hearts, for self-appraisal, and for good common sense, reasoning, and planning. (*Marriage and Divorce* [Salt Lake City: Deseret Book, 1976], pp. 12–13.)

Some couples may become unduly discouraged in marriage because they believe or have heard that others live their marriages in perfect harmony undisturbed by confrontations or differences in opinion. While some couples may eventually mature to that level, most of us are not that skilled, particularly during the early years of marriage.

With the hectic pace of contemporary living, many married couples ride roller coasters through life, at times experiencing ecstasy, at other times blandness, and at still other times discouragement and disappointment. Couples need to consciously switch their method of measurement from the low of the lows to the high of the highs. During the times of the lows, couples should try to recall the highs or pleasant times of the marriage. Constantly reminding themselves of their marital highs is especially important for newlyweds, whose highs and lows are often more pronounced than those of couples who have been married for years. They might ask themselves, What have the highlights of the marriage been so far? What brought them about? Could we create these or similar experiences again? The good news is that the highs are in our control.

If we plan for and create some good times in marriage, we will have something to cushion the lows when they occur. We'll also find that the lows generally become less frequent and the highs more frequent. By measuring our marriage by our highs and planning for and creating more of them, we immensely increase our capacity to stay in love. We'll probably find too that our marital difficulties are not all that bad when viewed in this balanced perspective. It was Socrates who noted, "If all our misfortunes were laid in one common heap whence everyone must take an equal portion, most people would be contented to take their own and depart." (Laurence J. Peter, *Peter's Quotations: Ideas for Our Time* [New York: William Morrow and Company, Inc., 1977], p. 206.)

MARRIAGES WILL BE TESTED

When speaking to an LDS group in California on marriage, I made an observation I hadn't made before. It is so obvious as to be easily overlooked, but I've been careful to emphasize it since: *Every marriage will be tried and tested in various ways.*

Marital trials and tests come in different ways and intensities. The only given is that they will come. They may be major tests or setbacks such as unemployment, sickness, or the death of a child. But most will likely be the smaller trials and tribulations, which include burnt toast or roast, heavy rain or deep snow, dirty socks or underwear left on the floor, a flat tire, a dead battery in the car, a crowded freeway, a stalled automobile, confusion about schedules, missed appointments, headaches, or "all of the above."

These stresses come from physical, environmental, and mental sources. However, the origins of the irritations, frustrations, and tests are not important. Every married couple has them. The main concern is how married couples choose to react. Our choices of how to deal with the various trials or setbacks are of major importance.

In the fall Susan and I like to drive around the Alpine Loop up Provo Canyon. On mountain slopes we often notice some bared roots of pine trees that are bowed and twisted by the winds and mountain storms. We notice that even the strong Rocky Mountain winds and storms cannot unearth these magnificent trees. Each burst of wind may make them sway or even on occasion make them bow to one side or the other, but all this seems to strengthen them on the very spot where the roots have taken hold.

How do these trees survive the constant buffeting? They have deep roots that grip the rocks and soil and only let go when the tree finally dies. But this growth and tenacity doesn't happen overnight. Strong roots to defy the storms are produced through constant buffeting by the winds. Maybe we should welcome the occasional winds of trials and disappointments. They may be necessary to help us develop strength of character and tenacity.

IN SICKNESS AND IN HEALTH

There is another aspect of marriage that we seldom talk about. Many wedding ceremonies either state or imply that we marry "in sickness and in health," suggesting we should be as equally devoted to each other when we are ill as when we feel well.

Looking back on twenty-five years of marriage, Susan and I have been fortunate to experience mostly good health. We and our children have made few trips to the doctor or hospital for anything other than colds and a few minor scrapes and cuts that required minor attention. During the few times Susan has been ill, I have been healthy enough to help her through her difficult days. And when I have been down with an occasional flu or cold, she has experienced good health sufficient to look out for my needs.

During one particular holiday season, several of the children took turns, it seemed, staying home a day or two with the flu. Then Susan began experiencing a little coughing and fever. A few days later Doug, our oldest son, got the four-day flu. We learned that the holiday seasons are truly a time for sharing. Between Christmas and New Year's, our eight-month old baby, Brandon, developed a cold that required another trip to the doctor and pharmacy. Susan got over her fever but could not get rid of her cough. During this time I did my duty by helping other family members.

Then it hit. One Sunday afternoon in January, I got a headache and started perspiring and wheezing. Doug brought by the 7-Up he had left over and wrote out when to take it and how much. He firmly believed 7-Up was a miracle drug. Susan was not yet better but felt that during those few weeks she had become somewhat of an authority on pain relievers. I assured them all I would be better by morning. But I was not.

Marriage is difficult enough when both partners are healthy. It becomes even more so when one or the other is ill. But what to do when both husband and wife are ill at the same time? Such was our situation that January when flu-ridden husband and wife sat up with an ill baby almost all night. Who should get up with a sick child is another topic in and of itself. But what do you do when both of you have a difficult time rolling out of bed for bottle warming and applications of liquid vitamins and Amoxin?

It's not so much who feels the best. It's who feels the least worse. When the baby cries, both of you wake up and then review your ailments out loud in an effort to show why you should not be the one to get up. But when your high temperature is offset by the other person's difficulty in breathing, you end up doing the sane thing. You take turns getting up with an ill child.

The next morning while lying in bed, I asked Susan, "What makes you feel the best when you are ill?

"Make-up," she replied. "Men do not understand that how a woman feels is greatly affected by how she looks."

I sat up in bed and wondered if a little blush and eye shadow really would clear up my head.

"Brent, why don't you get out of bed and help me clean the kitchen?" she inquired.

"It's because," I began, "I can't breathe, talk, and work at the same time."

"Why not just skip the talking and practice breathing and working?" she asked. Susan must not have watched any of those ads on television for cold medicines where wives pour spoonfuls of the stuff down hubby's throat and rub his back at the same time.

Susan did give me a hug while I was getting out of bed. I believe that those hugs and small acts of attention are what every husband and wife need to practice. Sickness is no fun at any time. But when you're both ill, you need to do some things in your marriage that you ordinarily wouldn't do. Along with the hugs and patience, we used medication and got lots of rest. (The data on the effectiveness of blush and eye shadow is not in.) You will probably find, as we did, that during times of sickness in marriage, husbands and wives need to be extraordinary in their sensitivity and attentiveness. Those are the times least suited for bickering, fault-finding, and hurt feelings.

MARITAL POTHOLES

In addition to illness, marital tension and stress can be experienced in a variety of ways. Conflict can arise over major issues such as whether or not to seek employment in another city. Conflict often occurs over major decisions like buying an automobile or buying a new or larger home. Most of us soon become aware of the areas of conflict in our marriage that cause us problems. But there is another dimension of the marital relationship when things do not go so well that we need to be aware of. I call it the marital potholes.

Not long ago Susan and I decided to drive over to American Fork to visit her mother. There are three ways to get from Orem to American Fork. We could take the "old road," the one that goes through Lindon and Pleasant Grove. Or we could take Eighth North down to the I-15 freeway. Still another option is to travel the back roads down by Utah Lake. This particular time we decided to go on the back roads, which takes more time but is a pleasant drive through the countryside.

We were driving along that evening, talking to each other and enjoying the fresh country air and the scenery. But apparently I was not paying enough attention to my driving. We hit a large pothole in the road.

As we recovered from the jolt, Susan asked, somewhat annoyed, if I wanted her to drive. I replied that I hadn't seen the pothole in time to avoid it. In my own defense, I commented that some potholes are unavoidable because they can't always be detected. She countered that the one I hit was both visible and avoidable. I tried in vain to disagree, and then the disagreement was over. The temporary stress in our marriage lasted little more than one minute, short but real. The momentary jolt of hitting the pothole caused some discomfort for both of us. The pothole was not particularly large or deep, certainly not large enough to cause much concern. The jar of the pothole was over almost as soon as it began, and we continued on that evening and enjoyed the remainder of the drive.

Sometimes in marriage, things seem to go well, and then we hit potholes of various kinds. They are the short, often unforeseen, and sometimes unavoidable aspects of life that cause momentary conflict or stress in marriage. Marital potholes are unique from other problems because they can't always be detected in advance and the origin is often unknown. In addition, we sometimes don't know why they upset us. But the fact is, they do.

Marital potholes create discomfort and sometimes cause momentary strained feelings. And they can be quite disruptive if we are traveling fast or hit a series of them in succession. But one pothole usually doesn't do much damage or last very long, particularly if we recognize its temporary nature. The impact is often over as quickly as it begins.

Potholes in life, either in marriage or on the road, can be survived if we are alert, have a tight grip on the steering wheel, maintain control, and keep our eyes on the road ahead. And not make a pit out of a pothole.

THE HUMPTY DUMPTY SYNDROME

During marriage, almost every married couple will face a few major crises. A crisis may be highly detrimental to the couple, or it may actually prove to be beneficial. You might wonder, "How could a crisis, trial, or major setback in life be beneficial?" I call the answer the "Humpty Dumpty Syndrome." As children, we recall repeating the Humpty Dumpty nursery rhyme many times:

> *Humpty Dumpty sat on a wall,*
> *Humpty Dumpty had a great fall.*
> *All the king's horses and all the king's men,*
> *Couldn't put Humpty together again.*

Many people are, indeed, like Humpty Dumpty. After a fall their life seems to be shattered. And like the horses and king's men, no one can seem to help them reconstruct their lives.

Why Humpty Dumpty couldn't be put back together is interesting. First, horses obviously aren't very good at reassembling broken eggs. And second, once an egg breaks, the shell is broken into many small pieces. Therefore, Humpty Dumpty remained shattered.

Some people, when they experience a major crisis in life, are not like Humpty Dumpty. The pieces of their life can be put back together. How these pieces are reassembled often makes the person, or couple, stronger, more resilient, and better able to cope with life. In their cases the crises eventually prove to be a blessing rather than a burden.

How well a person, couple, or family deals with a crisis depends on several things. First, what is the state of the emotional health of the person or persons prior to the crisis? Second, what is the nature, intensity, and duration of the crisis? And third, and perhaps most important, what is done about it once the crisis occurs? What are the crisis-coping skills? All these, plus the help sought in dealing with a crisis, contribute to the outcome and impact of a crisis in life.

When I was teaching college in Wisconsin, I had a graduate student in her late twenties who was doing very well. She told me one day that she married when she was in her late teens. And for reasons still unknown to her, her husband died just one year after their marriage. She understandably was devastated by the experience. She said she went into a major depression and had to seek professional counseling for several months. She related how she was eventually able to come to grips with her husband's death. She was also able to deal with many of her personal problems and concerns she had prior to her marriage.

As a result of the counseling she had, she said that she became a better, stronger person. She eventually remarried, had two children, and was then at the university pursuing a graduate degree. In her case she had carefully reassembled and put back together again the pieces of her life.

As newlyweds, remember that the crisis is not what counts the most. What you do about it is what really matters. (Unlike Humpty Dumpty, don't let horses help you with the reassembling process.) Consider whether you might be like my graduate student in Wisconsin. Even though you experience a painful, overwhelming event in life, you can emerge from it a stronger, better person or married couple. It all depends on the action you take afterward. And that is up to you.

CHAPTER 12

STAYING ON COURSE

Newlyweds today generally get a great start on their marriage. The ceremony, the wedding dinner, the reception, and the honeymoon are joyous occasions. Family and friends often come in great numbers to wish the new bride and groom well. They start off right on course.

But where will they be a month later? A year later? Five years later? Will they still be on course, or will they be drifting in the current turbulence of marital disruption?

I've always been amazed how airline pilots and navigators can reach their destinations right on the mark—and usually on schedule—when the destinations are so far away and unseen for most of the journey. I recently heard an interesting observation about planes and boats: they are usually off course 95 percent of the time. Only through the constant attention of the pilot, captain, and navigators are planes and ships constantly brought back on course during the journeys.

I think that's a wonderful analogy for newlyweds. If you are like most other married couples, you will likely drift off course, on occasion, in your efforts to have a rewarding and successful marriage. But commitment helps you get back on course and continue the journey. Just because you are off course does not necessarily mean the trip must be ended. Determine where you are now, compare it with where you want to be, and get back on course.

Some newly wedded couples eventually divorce or fail to stay in love because they experience a series of failures—times when they are off course. The disappoints could be financial or occupational. They could be related to education, health, children, or any other number of sources. The fact is, we all experience failures.

PARABLE OF THE SOWER

One of the interesting parables taught in the Bible is the parable of the sower. (See Matt. 13:3–8.) Jesus tells of a sower who went about scattering seeds. Not all of them grew because some fell on beaten paths or hardened soil, while others fell in stony places or among thorns. Only when the seeds fell on good ground, did they take root and bear fruit.

The parable was originally given in regard to the people's receptivity to the message of Jesus Christ. But there is another significant message contained in the parable: not everything we attempt to do in life is going to be successful; every seed we sow will not necessarily take root.

One interesting thing about the parable is that the sower had no way of determining in advance which of the seeds would take root and grow. But he labored to cast them about in hopes that at least a few would germinate and flourish.

Susan and I learned early in our marriage that we would experience many failures in life: not every job sought would be obtained; not every book written would be published; not every vacation carefully planned would be invigorating and refreshing; not every investment made would yield a return of 15 percent (if any); and not every car purchased would run smoothly for a hundred thousand miles or even past the warranty without adjustments and major repairs. Life would have many failures and setbacks.

We have also learned, however, that failure comes not only through unwise judgment, but also because of circumstances over which we have little or no control. We have learned some of our most valuable lessons in life through failure. But once we learned that failure was part of life, we've tried not to be unduly concerned. We keep casting our seeds in life with the faith and hope that some will take root—and they do. We eventually reap what we sow. (See Gal. 6:7.)

SEASONS OF GARDENING

In learning this valuable lesson about the law of the harvest, we have tried not to become preoccupied with the failures that surely come. Rather, we try to enjoy the occasional success. Rather than focus on the toil of the summer when the sun scorches the garden, the bugs attack, and some plants wither away and die, we have tried to focus on the harvest that will come.

The law of the harvest teaches us about the major seasons: *spring*, the time of planting and investing effort; *summer*, the time of nurturing and protecting; and *autumn*, the time of harvesting and reaping the reward of our efforts. But what about *winter*? What is it for, and when does it occur?

Most people believe that winter follows autumn and is a time for rest and recuperation. Others, however, believe that winter precedes spring and is a time of anticipation and preparation. Those people who have lived in a rural or farming community know that winter is a time to prepare for spring. It's the time we repair machinery and invest time and money in what we will need. And every winter is followed by a spring. That is a fact of life.

Perhaps you are presently in a nonproductive time of your marriage. Maybe you have had some failures in the recent past. During this time of your married life, you may see yourselves frozen into a way of life and living. As you huddle together, you believe that winter follows autumn.

Could there be better times ahead? If you and your spouse believe that winter precedes spring, you may prepare by repairing and investing for the vigorous growth that lies before you. Such is the law of the harvest. It applies to plants, and it also applies to people.

WHERE DO WE FOCUS IN LIFE

Some experts on human potential have made an interesting observation. They claim that only one out of every one hundred people is trained or is capable of dwelling on his positive attributes and successes. The other ninety-nine people tend to focus on their failures. They become preoccupied with what does not go well rather than with what does.

Some time ago I was asked to make some audiocassettes on marriage for SyberVision Systems in California. The president of the company, Steve Devore, told me he wanted something useful on marriage that he could market nationwide. The concepts had to be broad and general enough that almost any married couple of any ethnic, cultural, or socioeconomic background could benefit from them. I was also asked to create a workbook to go along with the six hours of audiocassettes.

It was quite a challenge, and I worked three months on the project. After the tapes and workbook were finally on the market under the title of *Successful Marriage*, I began to wonder if others would like and accept the audiocassettes. After a few months we began to see some results. I talked to one of the company representatives on the phone one day about the sales. He said that the program was selling about as expected. Then he mentioned, "Oh yes, about 10 percent of the cassettes are being returned for purchase refund."

After the call, I sat at my desk for a moment. Ten percent were being returned! I was stunned and, to be quite honest, very disappointed. I left the room and told Susan what I had just learned. The company offered a full sixty-day money-back guarantee on every product they sold. And apparently one out of every ten customers on my program were taking them up on their offer.

During the next few weeks the thought wouldn't go away. Ten-percent failure! I couldn't stop thinking about it. Finally, I called Steve DeVore on the phone and told him about my concern. He laughed and told me that if I were going into marketing, I would have to develop a new perspective on failure. Nationwide, he said, the return rate on similar audiocassette programs is about 30 percent with a thirty-day guarantee. The overall return rate for their company averaged about 20 percent with a sixty-day guarantee. He said they felt very good about their guarantee and the quality of their products. Since my program had only a 10-percent return, they felt the marketing was going very well. When I hung up, I had a new perspective of failure.

Not everything we do in life will work out or succeed. And we may perceive some things as failures that actually are not failures. There will be setbacks, but they should be compared with growth and accomplishments. Rather than focus on the 10-percent failure rate, I am now quite proud that 90 percent of the people are satisfied with the cassette programs on marriage. And I have become a little more philosophical—I want to be included in the one percent who focus on what goes right in life.

KEEP TRACK OF MARITAL SUCCESSES

The story is told of a great artist who painted a tiny picture of a bouquet of roses. The painting was magnificent. Never before, it seemed, had man executed so deftly a reproduction of nature. The picture was the envy of all artists who saw it and the despair of the lovers of art who yearned to buy it for their collections.

But the painter steadfastly refused to sell his work of art, saying, "Whenever I feel my hand has lost its cunning, whenever I doubt my ability, I look at my little picture of the roses and say to myself, 'You painted that. Your hand drew it. Your imagination conceived the colors. Your skill put the roses on the canvas.' Then I know that what I have done I can do again."

His philosophy of success was to hang on the walls of our minds the memory of our successes. We should take counsel of our strengths, not our weaknesses. We should think of the good jobs we have done, the times we rose above our average levels of performance and carried out ideas or dreams or desires for which we had deeply longed. Then we should hang these pictures on the walls of our minds and look at them as we travel on the roadways of life."

This story has significance for couples. As a marriage counselor I've noted that couples often become preoccupied with what has gone wrong with their marriage. Both husband and wife can rehearse, almost upon cue, all the failures and setbacks of their marital relationship. But if asked to recall some of the successes, some of the things they have done well, some obstacles they encountered and overcame, many couples have a difficult time identifying any.

While learning from our mistakes in marriage is important, we must keep them in perspective. If we continue to think of negative situations and failures, our behavior tends to follow suit. But the opposite is also true. If we tend to think of the more positive aspects of life, the things we have succeeded in doing, we, like the artist with his magnificent painting, are reminded of our strengths rather than our weaknesses.

Susan and I often catch ourselves playing a silly game. At the end of a long, difficult day, we start rehearsing all the things we intended to do but didn't get accomplished. One of us will start out by citing something left undone, and then the other follows. Unless we catch ourselves, we can go on and on.

One way we have found to stop this habit is to talk about the "dids" rather than the "did nots." Sometimes we amaze ourselves with what we actually did accomplish. Like most other married couples, we occasionally can stand back and admire our picture of roses.

Perhaps newlyweds should follow the advice of the artist concerning his painting: Focus on your strengths! When you do this, you will have a rich resource upon which to draw should you reach a point in your marriage when, individually or jointly, you begin to doubt your ability. Then you too can say, "If we've done it once, we can do it again." Then you can resolve to once more do what is needed.

YOUR MARITAL NET WORTH

About ten years after we were married, Susan and I decided we would sit down and determine our financial net worth. We had some instructions before us on how this was to be done. First, we wrote down the mortgage on our home and the money owed on our automobile. It was a sizeable amount. Then we added all our other debts, including credit card accounts and furniture payments. When we added up our list, we were quite discouraged. We had not realized that we had so many liabilities. As we looked over our list of debts, we talked about them for some time. It was a dismal feeling, to say the least.

Finally we looked at the instructions again, which suggested we make a list of what we owned—our assets. So we listed the market value of our home and cars, the approximate value of our furniture and household appliances at the time, and a few other items of value that came to mind. After adding up the list of assets, we subtracted the sum of our liabilities from the sum of our assets. The result was our financial net worth.

We found that even though we owed others a considerable sum of money, our assets were slightly greater. When all factors were considered, we found we were actually worth something financially. This exercise also taught us another valuable lesson about life, and particularly about marriage: *Liabilities must always be weighed against assets.*

When we were determining our financial net worth, we dwelt a long time on our debts or liabilities. If that was all we had looked at, we might have become unduly discouraged. Only after we had determined what we owned did the whole financial picture take on a different perspective. When compared to our assets, our liabilities didn't look quite so bad.

As a marriage counselor, I often get long lists from couples detailing what is wrong with their marriage — their marital liabilities. They tend to rehearse these at length and continuously talk about what has gone wrong in their marital relationship. I often suggest they refocus their attention on their marital assets: What is going well now or has gone well in the past? Do they regard their children as assets in their marriage? In addition, what have they invested thus far in the marriage in time, money, energy, and emotion? When couples concentrate on the positive aspects, the marital troubles — both imagined and real — seem less disruptive. When dealing with money and marriage, remember that liabilities must always be weighed against the assets.

Perhaps you and your spouse would like to complete one or two exercises pertaining to marriage and past successes. The first exercise is called "Determining Our Marital Net Worth," and the second is simply called "BAGS."

Determining your marital net worth. Under the column of "Liabilities," list some of your present concerns or problems in your marriage ("Work Areas"). Next, under the column of "Assets," list some of the accomplishments or successes you and your spouse have achieved thus far in your marriage. Marital assets might include such things as major and minor satisfactions derived from the marriage, your children, other activities you jointly enjoy, your home, some of your material possessions, education and jobs attained, and any crises or difficult experiences you have confronted and overcome in your marriage.

DETERMINING OUR MARITAL NET WORTH

Assets (Accomplishments)	Liabilities (*Work Areas*)
Examples	Examples
Stayed together ___ years	Need to spend more time together as a couple
One child	Too much time spent with family/friends
Survived serious illness of wife	More endeavor needed in spiritual area
Both committed to marriage	

Look at both lists and compare them. Which list is longer?

Can you remember anything else that should go on either list, particularly under Assets? (Remember, most naturally focus on liabilities.) Now consider the following equation: Assets − Liabilities = Net Worth.

Hopefully, you have more marital assets than liabilities. If not, don't worry. You'll just have to go to work and make more deposits to cover future withdrawals. Just remember:

(1) In determining your marital net worth, your liabilities must always be compared to your assets.

(2) Marital net worth improves by either "decreasing" your liabilities or "increasing" your assets, or both.

BAGS. The second exercise is called "BAGS," which is an acronym for *Blessings, Accomplishments, Goals,* and *Service.* You can do this jointly or individually. At the top of a clean sheet of paper, write "Blessings"; on a second page, write "Accomplishments"; on a third page, write "Goals"; and on a fourth page, write "Service." (See Denis Waitley, *Seeds of Greatness,* [New York: Pocket Books, 1983], p. 49.)

Now go through each page or topic and write down everything you have done, individually or jointly, in that area. Under "Blessings," write down the things that you have been given or that have come to you in life without your own efforts: health, a sound mind, the country in which you live, or anything else for which you are genuinely thankful. In essence, "Count Your Many Blessings"; literally, name them one by one. As you recall other blessings later, go back to your work sheet and record them.

Under "Accomplishments," write down anything you have attained or done well in life through your own efforts. Go back to your childhood and teen years. Did you win any awards or prizes for any outstanding efforts? Write them down! (In my BAGS list, I recorded that I scored sixteen points in a play-off game in basketball in 1956 at Gunnison Valley High School!) If you graduated from high school or college, write it down. What contributions have you made to your community in the past? Record everything you have accomplished in life of which you are justly proud.

Next, go to the sheet marked "Goals" and write down some things you want to accomplish or attain in the future. Again, you might do this as a married couple or as an individual. You might have some immediate goals you want to accomplish in the next few months. But what do you wish to accomplish five years from now? Ten years? Twenty years? After retirement?

And finally, what services have you rendered to others during your life up to now? Write these under "Service." This would include any church work or anonymous help rendered to a disabled or disadvantaged person. Review what you have done for your neighborhood or community. Include volunteer work or donations to organizations.

After you have started your BAGS list, add to each of the four columns as past events come to mind. Remember, your list is a marriage inventory, not for anyone else to see except you and your spouse. It is a reminder of the good and positive things that have happened to you in the past. It keeps life's accomplishments and failures in perspective.

When you experience a setback in life or a genuine failure of some kind, get out your BAGS list and read it. In reality, your list becomes your portrait of roses. And like that artist, you can look at it again and again and say to yourself, "I did it once . . . I can do it again!"

The admonition to dwell on positive things, including what happens in our marriages and families, is not new. The Apostle Paul told us to focus on the good things in life: "Whatsoever things are true, . . . honest, . . . just, . . . pure, . . . lovely, . . . of good report; if there be any virtue, and if there be any praise, *think on these things*." (Philip. 4:8; italics added.)

. . . .

CHAPTER 13

SOME THOUGHTS ABOUT DIVORCE

Many newlyweds may reach a point in the early years of marriage when they actually contemplate divorce. Unfortunately, society has become so divorce-prone that couples frequently marry today thinking that they have an unspoken escape clause written into the marriage contract. Divorce is so much in our thinking that many spouses bring up divorce during disagreements as a matter of course, even when they have no intention of separating. Here are a few thoughts to consider:

DON'T DECIDE ABOUT DIVORCE UNDER STRESS

Susan and I have had to make countless decisions together. Some of these decisions have been made wisely, with beneficial outcomes. Others have not. But we are learning. And one thing we have learned is not to make major decisions in life during times of stress. We learned this in part from our son's paper route.

When our son Jon was thirteen years old, he returned one summer evening from having completed his paper route. "This sure is a good job," he said as he got off his bicycle. "Delivering these thirty-eight papers takes less than half an hour. And it's pretty good money for the time involved."

Jon was right. Delivering the evening newspapers was a good job for him. Particularly in the summertime and during good weather. But on Sundays, he

133

had to deliver them in the morning, and during the winter months, we both had to get up at six so I could take him in the car to deliver the papers.

I recall one cold snowy Sunday during January. I woke Jon at 5:30 A.M. He was tired but got up anyway and put on his hat, heavy coat, gloves, and rubber boots. When he opened the front door, a gust of cold air blew in. We were greeted by nearly one foot of new snow swirling around in the bitter wind. Jon closed the door. "I don't know if the paper route is worth it," he said. "Look at the snow. Just open the door and feel how cold it is."

He was right about the cold. I didn't want to go out either. But we couldn't quit now, so I told him we would talk it over while delivering the papers. Jon agreed but kept grumbling about how unpleasant it is to deliver newspapers on cold winter days. He constantly questioned whether he should keep his paper route. We also got stuck once along the way, and Jon had to help push the car out of the snow. We finished the paper route and started for home. Should he quit or continue his paper route?

Finally I said to my young son, then numb with cold, "Jon, you should never make up your mind about a paper route during a snow storm."

What I meant was that major decisions should never be made during times of discomfort or stress. Jon and I then talked about the snow and how the worst would be over in a few weeks. We reminisced about the spring, summer, and fall seasons and about the way he felt during those times. He admitted that the job was much more pleasant then and that it was pretty good work for the time and amount of money involved.

Jon kept his paper route for another year until he gave it to his younger brother Jason. Both learned to whiz around the neighborhood on their bicycles, and by working only about thirty minutes a day, they earned most of the spending money they needed. They enjoyed the warm, pleasant months, but they also prepared for the winters.

Major decisions in life (for young boys or anyone) require plenty of time and thought. This is particularly true of decisions about getting into or out of marriage.

TALKING ABOUT DIVORCE

While we should be careful not to automatically think about divorce when difficulties arise in marriage, we should be even more cautious not to talk about it to our spouse. During the past few years, I have noticed an interesting trend. The frequency with which a couple talk about divorce often determines whether or not it will actually occur.

A married couple may experience a conflict that upsets and disturbs them. They might try to work it out, but their efforts seem futile. If the problem continues and the tension mounts, what should they do?

One common reaction is for either or both to mention divorce. At first, usually neither takes it seriously. It is just a thought. They may think that talking about divorce is understandable because it is so common. They constantly hear about it in the media. Perhaps they have had close friends or family members terminate their marriages. According to present-day attitudes (shared unfortunately by many Latter-day Saints), they think that if their own marriage takes a downswing, the logical thing to do is consider divorce.

For some couples, divorce may be the appropriate solution. As an LDS marriage counselor, it took me some time to concede that it is best for some individuals not to be married to each other. Abuse or neglect, for example, will destroy people rather than build them up. Addictions will strain marriages and create unhealthy relationships. And people can change in negative ways and become unbearable to live with after the marriage has occurred.

But I believe many couples divorce unnecessarily. They hit some snags or rough spots in life and decide to end their marriages. Sometimes the decision

135

to divorce just gradually eases into their thinking. It may not be so much what some couples want to do. They just can't think of any alternative.

I have found that we often gravitate toward our dominant thought patterns. This is the modern way of saying what was noted centuries ago: "For as he thinketh in his heart, so is he." (Prov. 23:7.) Earl Nightingale has become well-known and wealthy for effectively teaching six simple words: "We become what we think about."

If we become what we think about, then the more often we think and talk about divorce, the more likely we set ourselves up for it. If we let our minds wander during marital difficulty and frequently talk about separation, then separation becomes more of a probability for us.

Talk about divorce can begin innocently. Perhaps it is just a thought. Or, in a moment of anger, a husband or wife might threaten divorce as a means of getting back at a spouse. Just a threat, they may think later. But what if the partner in that argument or in later arguments counters with his or her own threat of divorce? Soon the couple is off to the lawyer's office because of something said in a moment of anger. Even idle mentions of divorce seldom stay idle. Emotional patterns have a tendency to escalate.

As I counsel couples in marriage, I suggest that they not mention divorce until *all* other alternatives have been explored and tested. If you are in a difficult situation right now in your own marriage, you can spend the time far more fruitfully and even happily by working to improve the marriage than by working to end it. Remember that you might bring about a divorce prematurely and unnecessarily just by talking about it so often.

IS THE GRASS REALLY GREENER ELSEWHERE?

During the course of a marriage, husbands and wives may sometimes wonder if they have made the right choice of partners. Many people who are displeased with their marriages often think that they could do better by leaving their spouses. Rather than working to improve their marriages, they feel that starting over with someone else is the answer.

During the past few years in the United States, marriage has been attacked from a variety of directions. Some have claimed that marriage is outdated while others note the value of being single to enjoy the freedom that supposedly comes with divorce. But does research indicate that this is so?

In his book *Helping Couples Change: A Social Learning Approach to Marital Therapy,* Dr. Richard Stuart has made some insightful, well-documented observations on both marriage and divorce. After a careful review of the literature, he notes, "The acid test of the wisdom of divorce can be found only in an assessment of its effects." (New York: The Guilford Press, 1980, p. 8.)

Dr. Stuart first reviews some of the positive results of divorce: "(1) A freedom from domestic routines; (2) an opportunity to rear children without the opposition of the other parent; (3) freedom from conflict with a troubled mate; (4) an opportunity to control one's own resources and life space; and (5) opportunities to make personally fulfilling choices without constraint through the need to consider the wishes of others." He then cautions, "But divorce is very far from an unmixed blessing" and notes the following findings from extensive research in the field of marriage and family:

1. "Many reviewers have found that the health of divorced, separated, and widowed adults is inferior to the health of those whose marriages remain intact. . . . Those who are married fare much better than those who are divorced, separated, or widowed on almost all categories."

2. "Married respondents have (1) lower mortality rates; (2) lower suicide rates; (3) lower rates of victimization through homicide; (4) lower rates of fatal auto accidents; and (5) decreased morbidity due to coronary diseases and cancer of the digestive organs." (P. 8.)

3. "Divorced persons have a significantly higher rate of mental disorders than their married counterparts. . . . When mental health differences do surface, they show the power of a tidal wave during a tropical typhoon, with risk rates of the formerly married exceeding those of the married by as much as 20-fold in certain categories."

4. "Family disruption resulted in an income loss on the order of 33% or more for men and some 16.5% for women. So great is the economic consequence of divorce . . . that divorce is a stronger correlate of poverty than is race." (P. 11.)

Someone once compared divorce to jumping off the Eiffel Tower. You first feel an initial sense of freedom, exhilaration, and liberation; but then you quickly face the consequences. Dr. Richard Stuart concludes:

> It is clear that broad trends greatly favor the continued health and well-being of those who sustain their marriages. . . . Divorce may be a liberating experience for two people who would have suffered emotionally, physically, economically, or otherwise had they remained together. But it can also signal the start of a gradual process of deterioration of these and other dimensions, with freedom bringing the potential for disaster much as it carries with it a hope for nirvana. . . .
>
> The tide seems to flow in the direction of marriage and familism, and efforts to improve troubled marriages move *with and not against* this tide.
>
> The existence of a stable marriage has many benefits. . . . It helps partners to carve out and to maintain a stable personal identity. It provides a foil for screening perceptions and motivations to improve their quality. It seems to enhance personal, professional, and social living and to reduce the pain of many physical and emotional stresses. (P. 11, 14–15.)

One national survey cited in *Helping Couples Change* concluded that "Marriage and family life are the most satisfying parts of most people's lives and being married is one of the most important determinants of being satisfied with life." (P. 15.)

I would urge Latter-day Saint newlyweds (or any couple, for that matter) who are seriously contemplating divorce to carefully read Dr. Diane Medved's book *The Case against Divorce* (New York: Donald I. Fine, 1989). The psychologist from California takes a courageous, persuasive, and long-overdue stand against divorce. She states her premise on pages ten and eleven:

> I write this book as a counterbalance, to shake a few shoulders, with hopes that I might spare some children helplessness and some partners pain. I want to expose the forces that strive to hide the damage of divorce. Too many people think "If only I could be out of this marriage . . . " and conclude that sentence with their own private miracles. To repeat: It's not their fault; they're victims of propaganda. But the lure lets them down, for after they buy it they inevitably remain the same people, with the same problem-solving skills, values, and styles of relating to another. And so they can't help but choose and shape new relationships into duplications of their spoiled romance. *How can they be expected to see that divorce is, with few exceptions, the wrong way to improve their lives?* (Italics added.)

She also says that we are often too tolerant of friends and relatives who are divorcing, trying to be understanding when in fact we are being blind:

> It's finally time to renounce — openly and clearly — these self-serving platitudes about independence and fulfillment and look at the reality of divorce. We act too frequently as if every infirm marriage deserves to die, based simply upon the emotional report of one distressed partner. Rather than viewing a separation first with alarm, we're full of sympathy for a divorcing friend, and we offer understanding of the temporary insanity involved in severing old ties.

Still influenced by the "do your own thing" era, we don't act constructively. We don't take the husband (or wife) by the shoulders and shake him. We don't shout in his ear that he might be making a disastrous mistake. Even if we care immensely about him, we feel it's too intrusively "judgmental" to do more than step back and say "Okay, if that's what you want," and close our eyes to the consequences. My research suggests that this is more cruelty than friendship. (P. 8.)

CAN PEOPLE LEARN TO LOVE EACH OTHER AGAIN?

I have often been contacted by individuals who have asked this question: If a husband and wife no longer love each other, is it possible for them to learn to love each other again? This is a compelling question, and the answer may determine the future of many marriages.

As noted early in this chapter, I am a firm believer that action generally follows thought or belief. This principle is critical to those husbands and wives who are wrestling with the question of renewing love. If they believe they can't love their spouses again, they won't. They may not even try. But if they believe they can—that loving each other again is possible—then at least they might try. Put another way, whether you believe you can, or believe you can't—you're right.

A close friend contacted me not long ago. She wrote a long letter indicating that she and her husband no longer loved each other and that they were seriously contemplating divorce. She then asked, "Is it possible for us to learn to love each other again?" Here are a few thoughts I sent in reply. (The names have been changed for obvious reasons.)

Dear Ann:

Thank you for sharing your concerns and feelings in your letter. I know it is difficult, but I admire you for doing it.

You and Phil undoubtedly face difficult days of decision ahead. I know your decision to either divorce or stay married will be made thoughtfully, carefully, and even prayerfully.

I shed a few tears after receiving your letter. Maybe it is because I do care a great deal about what happens to you, to Phil, and to your children.

You asked in your letter whether it is possible for the two of you to love each other again. That is a very difficult question but one about which I have strong feelings.

The answer is simply "yes." It is possible for you both to love each other again. Totally, deeply, and completely. Others have done it, and so can you.

You indicated that you have sought divine guidance through prayer on this matter. Another of the simple truths in life is this: "If thou canst believe, all things are possible to him that believeth." (Mark 9:23; see Matt. 17:20; Philip. 4:13.)

As Latter-day Saints we share similar religious values and believe in a second life, or a "life hereafter." We hope it will be spent with loved ones we now know. Most of us believe that the "next life" begins after death. (And in a real sense, you and Phil have experienced the death of your relationship.) But as my friend and associate Dr. Lynn Scoresby, a psychologist, has reminded so many people, this second life can begin during mortality. And it can begin with people with whom we are presently associated.

A new life together is possible for you and Phil, but it will take genuine belief, work, and effort. All things are possible. But you will determine whether or not it will occur.

Susan and I send our love and will think about you during the difficult days ahead. We value your friendship and will continue to do so in the future.

Sincerely,
Brent Barlow

CHAPTER 14

A TRIP TO TEMPLE SQUARE

Before we conclude this book on marriage for newlyweds, I would like you to come with me on a tour of Temple Square in Salt Lake City. You have likely been there before, but I would like you to go with me one more time.

By December of 1964 Susan and I had been dating several months. I wanted to ask her to marry me but didn't know where to go or what to say for the occasion. For some reason unknown to me at the time, I decided to take her to Temple Square. On December 31, New Year's Eve—a stormy winter evening—we drove from Provo to Salt Lake City. I parked the car near Temple Square, and we walked over and stood between the Handcart Monument and the Sea Gull Monument. After a few minutes I asked her to marry me.

She started to cry. At first I thought she was happy. But she continued to cry.

"Is there someone else?" I asked.

"There's got to be," she replied.

Finally she consented. So there we were: two young BYU students who loved each other but were naïve and unaware of the journey ahead. Susan and I have gone back to Temple Square many times and stood on that exact spot where we originally agreed to marry each other. Sometimes we are overwhelmed with what has happened to us.

We were married on June 5, 1965, and we both graduated from BYU. Since our wedding date, we have lived in thirteen apartments and homes in Utah, Florida, Illinois, and Wisconsin. I completed two advanced degrees, and Susan has worked either part- or full-time as an elementary school teacher. I have worked as an LDS seminary teacher at Davis High School in Kaysville, Utah; as an institute instructor at Tallahassee, Florida; and as a college professor at Southern Illinois University, University of Wisconsin-Stout, University of Utah, and finally Brigham Young University. During our twenty-five years of marriage, we both have lost a parent through death. Susan's father, Cecil Day, died in 1968, and my mother, Ruth Peterson, died in 1976. That New Year's Eve in 1964, when we decided to get married, we didn't anticipate the seven active and energetic children that would eventually come, bless our marriage, and introduce us to parenthood.

On our twenty-fifth wedding anniversary on June 5, 1990, Susan and I returned to that same spot on Temple Square. As we discussed both the past and the future of our marriage, I couldn't help but think about that sacred spot where it had all begun a quarter of a century before. I looked around and saw two monuments and two buildings that have become symbolic to us in our marriage. Perhaps they could be for others also.

THE HANDCART MONUMENT

First, there is the Handcart Monument depicting a husband, wife, and their children pulling their handcart across the plains on their way to the Salt Lake Valley. To us the Handcart Monument represents struggle and effort in making a marriage work.

When I taught at Southern Illinois University, I received a small grant to study the Mormon handcart pioneers. Susan and I traveled to Iowa City, where the handcart companies originated. We found the fields in which the

143

Mormon pioneers had camped in 1856 before leaving for the Salt Lake Valley. I read many of the journals of those who made the trip, which described the struggles and efforts of those early Saints. About that same time we found some large wheels off an old discarded Amish wagon near Carbondale, Illinois. We made our own handcart, and tried to build it to scale. The cargo box was three feet wide, four feet in length, and sturdy enough to hold five hundred pounds, all the worldly goods and possessions a family was allowed on the one-thousand-three-hundred-mile trek.

On more than one occasion when life has been hectic and somewhat difficult for us, we compare ourselves to the handcart pioneers. We think that we struggle now, but then we look at the many pictures and drawings we have collected over the years and realize that we just struggle in more comfortable ways.

We have come to appreciate the fact that marriage is not intended to be particularly easy. Not that we try to make it difficult. Life sometimes makes it that way. But we have agreed to tote our handcart in our generation and pull together to bear the burdens placed upon us.

President Spencer W. Kimball once made a comment that made the handcart analogy even more significant to Susan and me:

> We repeat for emphasis from Matthew: "Enter ye in at the strait gate." That's a s-t-r-a-i-t gate, not the shortest distance between two points. *Strait* means hard, difficult, exacting, that kind of a gate. And that's the kind of a gate that marriage is. An eternal marriage is also strait and difficult, but it's rewarding and beautiful. "Strait is the gate, and narrow is the way, which leadeth unto life, and few there be that find it." (Matt. 7:13–14.)
>
> Now, all Latter-day Saints are not going to be exalted. All people who have been through the holy temple are not going to be exalted. The Lord says, "Few there be that find it." For there are the two elements: (1)

the sealing of a marriage in the holy temple, and (2) righteous living through one's life thereafter to make that sealing permanent. *Only through proper marriage—and I repeat that—only through proper marriage can one find that strait way, the narrow path.* No one can ever have life, real life, in any other way under any other program. ("Marriage Is Honorable," in *Speeches of the Year, 1973* [Provo: BYU Press, 1974], pp. 265–66; italics added.)

THE SEA GULL MONUMENT

Directly north of the Handcart Monument is the Sea Gull Monument representing the event in 1848 when gulls rescued the pioneers by eating the crickets that were destroying the much-needed crops. To Susan and me, the Sea Gull monument has come to represent one important element needed in life. And that is hope.

I have stated on many occasions that every LDS couple I know is fighting crickets of some kind. It seems to be part of mortality. During our struggles as newlyweds and later on in marriage, Susan and I often wondered when the Lord would intervene in our lives and when he would allow us to struggle.

Throughout our journey from state to state during our marriage, we have experienced numerous difficult moments. We learned that truly it is sometimes the darkest . . . right before the storm! And like the Prophet Joseph Smith, we too have uttered the words, "O God, where art thou? And where is the pavilion that covereth thy hiding place?" (D&C 121:1.) I believe that every LDS couple offers that prayer on several occasions during their married life. We too petition for divine help with our daily struggles.

The question is why does the Lord sometimes let us struggle before assisting us? Why don't the sea gulls come immediately? I have been so intrigued with the sea gull and cricket episode in Church history that I have studied it closely, and I have found several interesting things.

Orson Pratt, John Brown, and a few others first entered the Salt Lake Valley on July 19, 1847. Note the contrasting irony of the following two journal entries of Orson Pratt. First he wrote, "We could not refrain from a shout of joy which almost involuntarily escaped from our lips the moment this grand and lovely scenery was within our view."

In the paragraphs to follow, Orson Pratt continued to write of the beauty of the Salt Lake Valley. Then he added one short, significant sentence: "We found the drier places swarming with very large crickets, about the size of a man's thumb." (Brigham H. Roberts, *A Comprehensive History of The Church of Jesus Christ of Latter-day Saints,* 5 vols. [Provo: BYU Press, 1965], 3:216, 219.)

I tell that story to newlyweds in my classes because I think it has a message. The crickets were there when the pioneers arrived. The Mormon men and women had faced difficulties and trials before they even entered the valley. But they drove down Parley's and Emigration canyons and made their homes. It was said of the Mormon pioneers that they went west willingly because they had to. They had no choice because the Lord was depending on them.

The same is true of young couples marrying today. In real ways they are still pioneers looking down into the valley. They look around at the difficulty and disruption in many homes in the nation and world. Still, they too march down into the valley to start their homes and family life. And they do it willingly. The Lord and others are depending on them. Yes, there will be crickets to fight, but the sea gulls are on standby alert.

When studying the sea gull and cricket incident, I also learned another valuable lesson about marriage and family life. The crickets attacked the crops early in the spring of 1848, but the sea gulls did not arrive immediately. Why? Does the Lord expect us to actually fight crickets? More than once when Susan and I have had some difficult moments, we looked out on the horizon and saw a symbolic bird approaching. We hoped it was a sea gull. In an unusual twist of events, it sometimes turned out to be a buzzard. We saw what we thought was the light at the end of the tunnel, and it turned out to be another freight train heading our direction. But our experience and testimony are that the sea gulls are right behind the buzzards and freight trains. The Lord will never let his covenant people go under. Struggle, yes. But never go under.

Someday I would like to write a book titled *Between the Crickets and the Sea Gulls,* or *What to Do until the Sea Gulls Arrive.* It would deal with that difficult period between the time we make our petitions for divine assistance and the time when it finally comes. One time in the late 1970s, Alex Haley, author of *Roots,* came to the BYU campus to speak. He told a story that, in a way, has to do with crickets and sea gulls. Alex Haley said that his grandmother had once taught him something about when the Lord helps and when he doesn't. She told him, "God doesn't come every time you call, but when he does come, he is never late."

Perhaps that is the answer to crickets, sea gulls, and contemporary life. The Lord may want us to struggle some, for what purpose we're not always sure, but he will never let us down. It is not so much *if* he will assist, but *how* and *when.* The Lord has assured that he will help, but he will do it in his own due time. (See Eccl. 3:1; D&C 43:29.) A recent bride once told me about the importance of hope, of anticipating better times ahead. She said that she and her husband had married with the highest hopes and dreams of a happy marriage. But shortly after their marriage in the Logan Temple, the crickets attacked. In hordes. Her husband became ill and had to drop out of school. She became pregnant, had a miscarriage, and also had to quit her education. Her husband became so ill that he couldn't work. Against their desires, they had to live first with his parents, and later with hers. They had to receive financial assistance from the Church for several months until he was well enough to find work, then finally continue on with his education.

The young wife, now with a little baby daughter, told me that there was one verse of scripture they read often during those difficult years of marriage: "Search diligently, pray always, and be believing, and all things shall work together for your good, if ye walk uprightly and remember the covenant wherewith ye have covenanted one with another." (D&C 90:24.)

The scriptures also teach that love bears and endures "all things." (1 Cor. 13:7.) Our thirteenth Article of Faith states, "We have endured many things, and hope to be able to endure all things." What better way is there to bear and endure difficult moments in marriage than by believing and hoping?

THE TABERNACLE

Directly north of the Handcart Monument and the Sea Gull Monument is the Mormon Tabernacle. It was built in 1868. The Tabernacle might simply represent "community."

In a real sense, we need each other. We need the person we married, but we also need a continued relationship with family, friends, neighbors, church members, and others in the community. I have often cautioned newlyweds to carefully choose their friends and associates during the early years of marriage. Carefully select those with whom to build a "community," because those people will have a great impact and, in some cases, may greatly affect the outcome of the marriage.

This is particularly true during times when a couple may be contemplating separation. Couples who are on the brink of divorce go through a subtle socializing process. Many in their "community" may influence them negatively, and the couple may in turn influence their community negatively. I have seen it happen many times. One married couple will be unhappy and share their disappointments with another married couple. The second couple, in turn, become involved to some degree and start looking more critically at their own relationship. Sooner or later, usually sooner, both couples start gravitating toward divorce.

If you are disgruntled with your new marriage, avoid others in the same situation. Avoid telling friends or family members just how bad things are. If you find a sympathetic or empathic ear to encourage your verbal depiction of troubles, matters could become worse. And what's more, sometimes an unwise bond forms if the listener is of the opposite sex. Keep in mind that adultery often results more from empathy than from lust.

During your early years of marriage, and for the rest of your marriage for that matter, select a community of friends who themselves are happily married or are at least committed to the concept of marriage. That is one of the great things about our church. It is both a local and worldwide community to which each member can belong. We call each other "brother" and "sister." We come together to symbolically break bread and eat and drink together—the sacrament. We meet together often regarding the welfare of our souls (see Moro. 6:5), and by the very nature of our baptismal covenants, we agree to bear one another's burdens, comfort those who stand in need of comfort, and mourn with those who mourn (see Mosiah 18:8–10). We Latter-day Saints, of all people, should build "community" because we understand how much we truly need each other.

THE TEMPLE

The last edifice we will look at on our trip to Temple Square as newlyweds is the Salt Lake Temple. It stands as a visual link between this life and the next. It reminds us of eternity. As Paul noted, "If in this life only we have hope in Christ, we are of all men most miserable." (1 Cor. 15:19.)

I have asked many young Latter-day Saints why they want to marry in the temple. They usually give only one or two answers. The first is something like "So we can be together forever," and the second is "It is such a beautiful place." As far as getting married in a beautiful place, that is understandable. The LDS temples are beautiful. But there are other beautiful places in the world to get married. Some of the early Saints were married on Ensign Peak near Salt Lake City with the sweeping mountains and forests to surround them.

Whenever we talk of "eternal" marriage, we think only in the time dimension: forever. Is our goal only to be with someone forever, regardless of the nature of the relationship? In Doctrine and Covenants 19:7–12, the Lord explained to Joseph Smith the meaning of the word *eternal* in the phrase "eternal punishment." The Lord revealed, "Endless is my name. Wherefore— eternal punishment is God's punishment. Endless punishment is God's punishment." In a similar way, eternal marriage is not only one that lasts forever, but also one that has the *quality* of godliness. Eternal marriage means godly, God-like, or Christ-like marriage. It is one that has the potential to endure forever, bringing warmth, fulfillment, and growth to the couple and their children. I cannot think of anything less appealing than being together forever with someone I do not care deeply about. I want to have a quality, Christ-like relationship with my wife and children.

I also ask both singles and newlyweds at BYU if temple marriage and eternal marriage are synonymous. Can you have one without the other? If two people marry in the temple, never return, and are less than Christlike to each other, do they have a temple marriage? Technically, they have been married in the temple, so "yes," they do have a temple marriage. But we learn in the temple that we must apply or practice what we learn and covenant. There must be an application aspect of temple marriage.

Another key question. Is eternal marriage a process, an event, or both? We often talk of "getting married in the temple"—an event. But I also like to think of it as a process whereby we apply principles taught in the temple on a day-to-day basis. Actually eternal marriage is both. It is a process that begins with an event. Without the event, the process couldn't begin. And we need to return to the temple often to understand or remind ourselves what the process entails. We need to be reminded that temples are the link with both the past and the present, with mortality and the other side of the veil. As our children grow and mature, we need to be reminded that there is and can continue to be joy in our posterity. This is particularly important because the rigors of mortality may cause us to think otherwise.

ACRES OF SPIRITUAL DIAMONDS

A young LDS woman drove down from Salt Lake City a short time ago to see me. I had recently spoken in her stake on marriage, and she came, she said, to thank me for telling a particular story. She said it triggered the transition from her decision to divorce to her decision to stay married. You may have heard the story before. It is called "Acres of Diamonds."

Have you have ever heard of the Golconda Diamond Mine near the Indus River in India? It has produced some of the world's largest and most magnificent diamonds, including the crown jewels of England and Russia. How the mine was discovered was made famous by Russell Herman Conwell, a Protestant minister who traveled the world with his famous lecture "Acres of Diamonds." Conwell gave the lecture more than six thousand times in the United States and abroad, and, through that, he raised seven million dollars for the education of students at Temple University, which he founded in Philadelphia during the 1880s.

During November 1988 I flew to Philadelphia for a convention on family life. I took my twelve-year-old son, Jason, with me. One afternoon we decided to visit Temple University, and while we were there, I went to the University

book store and asked for a copy of the official version of "Acres of Diamonds."
They gave me the booklet *Acres of Diamonds: A Man, a Lecture, a University*,
a short history of Temple University and its originator, Russell H. Conwell.

According to Conwell, a farmer named Ali Hafed who lived near the
River Indus heard that others were becoming wealthy with their discoveries
of diamonds. Ali sold his farm, left his wife and children, and went in search
of diamonds. He traveled into Palestine, wandered all over Europe, and finally
died . . . in abject poverty in Barcelona, Spain. The man who purchased Ali
Hafed's farm later discovered that it was literally covered with diamonds —
acres of diamonds — and he became a wealthy man. The Golconda Diamond
Mine was later established on Ali Hafed's land.

Had Ali remained where he was and learned to recognize diamonds in
the rough, he would have become one of the wealthiest men in the world.
Instead, he left his home, his farm, and his family in search of wealth elsewhere.

I like to tell the story because I think it has an overriding spiritual message.
I often wonder what we leave at home in order to acquire the things in the
world. How many of us have left our own "acres of diamonds" with regard to
marriage and family in order to pursue other interests? Are too many of us
like Ali Hafed, thinking happiness and wealth will always be found somewhere
else? When Russell H. Conwell told the story, he encouraged the listeners to
stay where they were and look for success and wealth right in their own
community. And many did.

The scriptures, ancient and modern, give interesting admonitions relating
to the theme of "acres of diamonds." What do we give up of a spiritual nature
in pursuit of temporal things? Jesus asked, "For what shall it profit a man, if
he shall gain the whole world, and lose his own soul [or spouse, or family]?
Or what shall a man give in exchange for his soul?" (Mark 8:36–37.) Also,
if we remain faithful to gospel principles and covenants, we are promised, "He

that receiveth me receiveth my Father; and he that receiveth my Father receiveth my Father's kingdom; therefore *all that my Father hath shall be given unto him.*" (D&C 84:37–38; italics added.)

Each one of us should carefully evaluate our own "acres of diamonds." There are three basic spiritual lessons I think we can learn from the story: (1) I believe that most of us can find peace, contentment, and happiness in life with our present marriage partner. (2) Learning the lesson of Ali Hafed, we should know what have, what we would leave if we moved on. We may be leaving our own acres of diamonds. (3) We should learn to recognize diamonds in the rough that are uncut and unpolished.

This last thought was what brought the woman from Salt Lake City to see me. I had suggested that everyone has a spiritual nature that often goes unnoticed. The worth of each soul is, indeed, great. (See D&C 18:10.) So precious are we all — ourselves, our spouses, and our children — that Jesus Christ came to this world and gave his life for each one of us. That is how much we each mean to him! But in the day-to-day, humdrum existence of life, or because of the more trying and painful experiences, we fail to note or remember that each of us is a spiritual diamond in the rough, uncut and unpolished. But through toil and effort, the spiritual brilliance of each might yet be discovered.

In March 1832 the Lord made this promise: "Ye are little children, and ye have not as yet understood how great blessings the Father hath in his own hands and prepared for you; *and ye cannot bear all things now; nevertheless, be of good cheer, for I will lead you along. The kingdom is yours and the blessings thereof are yours, and the riches of eternity are yours.*" (D&C 78:17–18; italics added.)

Susan and I would like to invite all married couples, especially the newlyweds, to return to Temple Square often. Stand between the Handcart

Monument and Sea Gull Monument. Do it particularly if you are having difficult moments in your marriage. And most important, do it if you are seriously thinking of ending your marriage by divorce or separation.

Look at each of the following and think of these words:

Handcart Monument: struggle, effort, sacrifice (reread President Kimball's comments on marriage being the s-t-r-a-i-t gate).

Sea Gull Monument: hope and belief. (Reread D&C 90:24.)

Tabernacle: community. (Reread Mosiah 18:8–10.)

Temple: eternity. (Reread D&C 78:17–18.)

The promise is, that if we are faithful, the riches of eternity will be ours. We, too, can have our own acres of spiritual diamonds. It is written, "Eye hath not seen, nor ear heard, neither have entered into the heart of man, the things which God hath prepared for them that love him." (1 Cor. 2:9.)

A TEARFUL TRIBUTE

March 21, 1991, is a day I will never forget. It was the day our oldest son, Doug, was married to Becky Borden. The occasion was a joyous and yet sentimental one for both Susan and me and Bob and Neva Borden, parents of the bride. The marriage was the first of any son or daughter in either the Barlow or Borden family. (As this book goes to press, my daughter Tammy has announced her engagement. Susan and I extend to her our well-wishes for her forthcoming marriage.)

On the morning of the wedding in the Salt Lake Temple, we had a wedding breakfast. Bob Borden and I were invited to pay tributes to our son and daughter as they commenced their married life. I have given hundreds of lectures to thousands of students on the importance of and preparation for marriage. But now this was my own son and his soon-to-be bride to whom I had to speak.

What would I tell this young couple whom I dearly loved, just a few hours prior to their marriage? Finally, I decided to read to Doug and Becky a poem by Jan Struther called "Epithalamium: Marriage as an Act of Creation" (an epithalamium is a poem or song in honor of the bride and groom). After Bob gave his fitting tribute, I started to read, maintaining my usual stoic manner, but halfway through the poem, I became tearful. I apologized later for my sentimentality, but really, I enjoyed the tearful moment. I knew of nothing more fitting for the occasion than what I was trying to read.

Here is the poem, which I would like to share with all newlyweds as they begin their married life together:

The raw materials of love are yours . . .
Fond hearts, and lusty blood, and minds in tune:
And so, dear innocents, you think yourselves
Lovers full-blown.

Am I, because I own
Chisel, mallet and stone,
A sculptor? And must he
Who hears a skylark and can hold a pen
A poet be?
If neither's so, why then
You're not yet lovers. But in time to come
(If senses grow not dulled nor spirit dumb)
By constant exercise of skill and wit,
By patient toil and judgement exquisite
Of body, mind and heart,
You may, my innocents, fashion
This tenderness, this liking, and this passion
Into a work of art.

INDEX